NAME ABOVE ALL NAMES

NAME
Above All
NAMES

*Jesus Christ
Our Savior and Lord*

DAN HAYDEN

CROSSWAY BOOKS

A DIVISION OF
GOOD NEWS PUBLISHERS
WHEATON, ILLINOIS

Library of Congress Cataloging-in-Publication Data
Hayden, Dan, 1940-
   Name above all names / Dan Hayden
     p. cm.
   ISBN 1-58134-543-7 (TPB : alk. paper)
   1. Jesus Christ—Name—Meditations. 2. Bible. O.T. Isaiah IX, 6—
Meditations. I. Title.
BT590.N2 H39   2004
232—dc22   2003019732

CH		14	13	12	11	10	09	08	07	06	05	04
15	14	13	12	11	10	9	8	7	6	5	4	3	2	1

*Affectionately dedicated to the memory of
my father*

"Bob"
ROBERT D. HAYDEN
(1914-1995)

*who
first taught me that Jesus Christ
is the answer
to life and the life after life*

CONTENTS

1

NOT LIKE ANY OTHER

The Uniqueness of Christ in a Pluralistic World

For a child will be born to us,
a son will be given to us . . .
ISAIAH 9:6

Can two mutually exclusive things both be right at the same time?

"Well, what kind of a question is that?" you might ask. "Of course not—especially if the things are truly mutually exclusive. Black, if it is really black, cannot at the same time also be white—that would be a confusion of logic. It would also be a confusion of reality because that's not the way things are. Our world is full of contrasts and opposites: Men are not women, and women are not men. That's what makes life so interesting."

Today, though, that bit of logic is being challenged by our postmodern culture. *Postmodern* simply means that the rules of communication have been changed. The modern world of reason and logic has given way to a whole new age of flux and flow. Things aren't always what they seem, and mutually exclusive ideas can now both be considered true. No longer is truth "*the* truth." Truth can be whatever you want it to be. So you can have your truth, and I can have my truth; and even though we have opposite ideas, we can both be right. Isn't that nice?

The Fantasy World of Pluralism

Well, the idea that a plurality of ideas can all be right at the same time is called pluralism; and pluralism is the monster child of postmodern thinking. Pluralism has reduced life to an experience in which we really don't think anymore. Dracula is alive and well in our western culture—only he now goes by the name of Pluralism. This philosophy is a monstrous evil that is sucking the very lifeblood of reality out of our system. Our culture has become delusional, so that it is no longer strange to think that black is white and women are men. It's an upside-down world, and we've begun to see it as normal.

This is especially true in the area of religion. Mathematics and the hard sciences are still having a difficult time adjusting to pluralism as a worldview. You see, you can't put a man on the moon or cure cancer with pluralism. But when it comes to religion and spiritual matters, pluralism is the postmodern answer to the ideas and beliefs that divide us. If we can all be right, so the reasoning goes, then nobody can get upset, and we can all live happily ever after. It's the ultimate solution to peace in our world.

In September 1993 religious leaders from around the world converged on Chicago at the Parliament of the World's Religions. They met with a threefold purpose: to promote cooperation among the world's religious institutions, to renew the role of the religions of the world in relation to personal spiritual growth, and to develop interfaith programs that would continue religious cooperation into the twenty-first century. Attending the event, which was held one hundred years after the first parliament (also in Chicago), were Baha'is, Buddhists, Confucianists, Hindus, Jains, Jews, Muslims, Native Americans, Shintos, Sikhs, Taoists, Unitarians, Zoroastrians, as well as Protestants and Roman Catholics.[1]

Behind all the activities and meetings was a single major theme: religious pluralism, which says that the religions of the world may appear diverse on the surface, but if you boil them down to the basics, they are all really saying the same thing. It reminds me of *I'm OK, You're OK,* that seventies-era book of self-help psychology that said that despite all the surface differences between individuals, we are all basically the same, and we are all basically OK.[2] Religious pluralism says much the same thing—that when it comes to "God," we are all OK because, one way or another, all religious roads eventually lead to "God."

A year earlier, in June 1992, an international group of eighty-five evangelical theologians from twenty-eight countries met in Manila, Philippines, with the World Evangelical Fellowship to discuss the above-mentioned upcoming parliament. Their theme was entirely different, however, as they met to discuss "The Unique Christ in Our Pluralistic World." In 1995 Baker Book House published their work in a book with the same title. "Evangelical leaders are alarmed by the increasing religious pluralism and syncretistic influence within and outside the church," said Bong Rin Ro, the WEF Theological Commission Director, in the book's Foreword. "Moreover, this religious pluralism has crept into the evangelical church in a subtle way in recent years to cause divisions among evangelical Christians and to arouse theologians to be concerned."[3]

These evangelical leaders also drafted a document titled "The World Evangelical Fellowship Manila Declaration," and I would like to highlight a statement from it. Pluralists "claim that all religious beliefs are more-or-less equally valid and equally true. . . . Against such pluralism, we affirm that God has acted decisively, supremely, and normatively in the historical Jesus of Nazareth. In his person and work, Jesus is unique such that no one comes to the Father except through him. All salvation in the biblical sense of eternal life, life in the Kingdom, reconciliation with God and forgiveness of sins come solely from the person and work of Jesus Christ."[4]

So why talk about a pluralistic parliament from years ago? Because in my view this event helps us focus on what really is important *today*. This is the crucial issue, perhaps more crucial than any other religious issue of our times. "Christology," wrote Bruce Nicholls in the Introduction to the book from the Manila conference, is at "the centre of the storm. The central theological issue of our times is the Christological one."[5]

In the early 1980s I saw this trend toward pluralism beginning to take hold. So my wife, Karilee, and I established an organization called Christolized Ministries to share studies and present seminars that would draw attention to the importance of keeping Christ central in life and ministry. Because of the New Age emphasis on crystals, that name has fallen on hard times now; but the importance of the centrality and preeminence of Christ as the unique Savior is no less crucial in the twenty-first century than it was when we first founded Christolized Ministries. It is precisely during these pluralistic times that we must be strong on the basic elements of the Gospel: salvation by Christ alone, salvation by grace alone, and salvation by faith alone.

It is because of my concern for our understanding of the uniqueness of Christ during this moment in history that I have decided to publish these studies, which were first delivered as a seven-part sermon series during a Christmas season several years ago.

The Scripture we will be using is Isaiah 9:6, that favorite Christmas passage which reads:

> *For a child will be born to us, a son will be given to us;*
> *And the government will rest on His shoulders;*
> *And His name will be called Wonderful Counselor, Mighty God,*
> *Eternal Father, Prince of Peace.*

These seven studies come primarily from this one verse. We will take it phrase by phrase. We will look at it name by name. My approach to this endeavor is taken from Isaiah 28:10: "For it is precept upon precept, precept upon precept, line upon line, line upon line, here a little, there a little" (ESV). So let's examine Isaiah and his times, and then make application to some of the challenges we face in our modern world.

We Are Living in a Critical Time of History

As we look for answers to the world's problems, it should be obvious that we will not find them by following the rabbit down the hole into Alice's Wonderland. There everything is surreal and topsy-turvy—not at all like things in the real world. Answers can be whatever you want them to be in Wonderland, but they will not at all fix things in the land of reality.

Pluralism may say that all answers are equally valid and that no truth is "true" truth; but even Alice knows that this is craziness and not at all the way it was meant to be. In the real world things are right and wrong, and true and false, and wise and stupid, and up and down, and on and off. There are laws and rules that must be followed, and there are consequences when we mess up. Now that's the way it *really* is. And in the *real* world Christ is unique, and pluralism is a figment of the imagination.

As we begin looking at Isaiah's prophecy we discover that this prophecy, like all others, is set in a real-life situation. You will notice that Isaiah 9:6 begins with the little word "for"— "*For* a child will be born to us, a son will be given to us." This word "for" is a translation of the Hebrew conjunction *chi*, which is a connective word linking what is about to be said with what has already been said. In other words, we are invited to back up and see Isaiah's great prophecy about Christ in the *general context* of Isaiah's prophetic writings, and then specifically in light of the *immediate context* of chapter 9.

So we go back to the beginning. The book of Isaiah was written around 700-680 B.C. and was addressed to the people of the southern tribe of Judah during the time when God's people were divided into two separate governmental spheres, the northern kingdom and the southern kingdom. Addressing the southern kingdom of Judah, Isaiah begins with some unflattering remarks for his audience:

> *1 The vision of Isaiah the son of Amoz, concerning Judah and Jerusalem which he saw during the reigns of Uzziah, Jotham, Ahaz, and Hezekiah, kings of Judah. 2 Listen, O heavens, and hear, O earth; for the* LORD *speaks, "Sons I have reared and brought up, but they have revolted against Me. 3 An ox knows its owner, and a donkey its master's manger, but Israel does not know, My people do not understand." 4 Alas, sinful nation, people weighed down with iniquity, offspring of evildoers, sons who act corruptly! They have abandoned the* LORD, *they have despised the Holy One of Israel, they have turned away from Him.*
>
> —ISAIAH 1:1-4

These scathing words give us a picture of the spiritual state of the people of Judah during Isaiah's ministry, and it was very bad. The people had revolted against God, had shown less sense than the ox and donkey, and were a sinful, corrupt people who despised "the Holy One of Israel."

Rebellion against God has consequences, and several chapters later Isaiah warns Judah and Jerusalem of coming disaster: "The LORD will bring on you, on your people, and on your father's house such days as have never come since the day that Ephraim separated from Judah, the king of Assyria" (7:17). Here Isaiah recalls the rebellion described in 1 Kings 12 that resulted in the nation being divided into the kingdom of Israel (also known as Ephraim) in the north and the kingdom of Judah in the south. Eventually this division spelled disaster for the northern kingdom of Ephraim.

So here's Israel's plight: Isaiah is writing to the southern kingdom of Judah, reminding them that their northern brethren had become so bad that God had separated them out, the nation of Assyria had come down and taken them captive, and they were scattered throughout the world. That had happened in 721 B.C. (the destruction of Samaria and Israel), and now Isaiah's warning to Judah and Jerusalem is simply this: "Listen—if you keep going the way you're going, if you keep behaving as badly as your brothers behaved, the same thing is going to happen to you. Dark days, troubling days, are going to come upon you, just like Ephraim to the north."

Moving beyond chapter 7, Isaiah continues to relate the plight of God's people in chapter 9. He describes the "gloom" of a people who are "in anguish" (v. 1) and depicts the Israelites as a "people who walk in darkness" and who "live in a dark land" (v. 2) while under "the yoke of their burden" and subject to "the rod of their oppressor" (v. 4). Grievous affliction! Darkness, gloom, and anguish—truly difficult times. Wow! What a time God is predicting for these people!

It reminds me of that quartet on the old *Hee Haw* TV program. With downcast faces they would sing, "Gloom, despair, and agony on me! Deep, dark depression—excessive misery. If it weren't for bad luck I'd have no luck at all. Gloom, despair, and agony on me!" Well, that could have been Israel's song. In effect the people sang those lyrics for hundreds of years throughout centuries of dominion by the Gentile nations.

Now what was God's answer to this gloom and agony? As we read on, we see that the answer is *a great light:* "The light will shine on them" (v. 2). Gloom and despair will not have the final word because a great light will dispel the gloom and shine through the darkness. This was the hope of Israel.

The important question then is, *what or who is this great light?* Well, Matthew in his Gospel tells us that Jesus is that light. Quoting from this prophecy in Isaiah 9, Matthew applies it to Jesus at the beginning of His ministry:

> *12 Now when He heard that John had been taken into custody, He withdrew into Galilee; 13 and leaving Nazareth, He came and settled in Capernaum, which is by the sea, in the region of Zebulun and Naphtali. 14 This was to fulfill what was spoken through Isaiah the prophet, saying, 15 "THE LAND OF ZEBULUN AND THE LAND OF NAPHTALI, BY THE WAY OF THE SEA, BEYOND THE JORDAN, GALILEE OF THE GENTILES— 16 THE PEOPLE WHO WERE SITTING IN DARKNESS SAW A GREAT LIGHT, AND TO THOSE WHO WERE SITTING IN THE LAND AND SHADOW OF DEATH, UPON THEM A LIGHT DAWNED." 17 From that time Jesus began to preach and say, "Repent, for the kingdom of heaven is at hand."*
>
> —MATTHEW 4:12-17

Matthew is making the point that Jesus grew up in the town

of Nazareth, which was in Zebulun; and the center of His Galilean ministry was in the city of Capernaum, which was in Naphtali. As Jesus lived and ministered in these areas of Israel, He presented himself as the Messiah who would bring deliverance and hope to the people. *He* was the light of Isaiah's prophecy, the One who would dispel the darkness and inaugurate a new age for the nation.

Unfortunately, the nation of Israel rejected Jesus as their Messiah, and so the time of deliverance was delayed. Nevertheless Jesus predicted that He would return again in great power and glory (Matt. 24:29-31), and at *that* time Isaiah's prophecy will find its ultimate fulfillment. The "government" will finally be placed upon the shoulder of the Child who was born (Isa. 9:6), and peace will finally come to Israel (Isa. 9:7).

You see, it was a crucial time in Israel's history when Isaiah penned these words. But the answer to Israel's dilemma was in a Child who would be born; and that is our hope as well. As one thinks about it, *we* are living at a critical time of history too. Those who know anything about prophetic events and the biblical chronology of the end-times know that the last days of this age are very likely upon us.

Terrorism at home and abroad has become a major concern as multinational armies police the hot spots of the world. As a result, the geopolitical structure of the world seems to be in a major state of flux as nations struggle for survival on one hand and for supremacy on the other. For instance, Europe is emerging as a shooting star among the nations, while America is becoming increasingly isolated and marginalized in the arena of world affairs. Israel continues to be in the spotlight with very few friends and an enormous weight of pressure to conform to world opinion. The moral infrastructure of the western world continues to decline, and potential environmental disasters remain hot topics of concern. Looking at the big picture, prophetically significant things are happening. Actually it is all quite mind-boggling, and the thing most people want after watching the evening news is an aspirin for their headache.

So how do we find our way out of all this gloom and darkness? Well, the answer is not in some abstract theory, governmental philosophy, or outworking of events on the world stage. The answer for us is the same as it was for Israel in the prophecy of Isaiah. The answer is in a Person. The answer is in a Deliverer. The answer is in a Child who is born and a Son who is given. The answer is in Jesus Christ, the unique Savior of the world. We are living in a critical time of history, and the answer is a Person.

WE ARE LOOKING FOR A SPECIAL PERSON TO SAVE US

Isaiah is very specific. What will save us is a special Person: a Child, a Son. Salvation will not come in the form of a great idea, nor will it be found in some new philosophy of government. Our only hope is in a Person—*that* is what Isaiah is saying in Isaiah 9:6.

Our world seems to understand this. In her book *The Hidden Dangers of the Rainbow*, Constance Cumbey tells of a New Age claim that the person who would save the world had been found. In the preface of her book she tells the story:

> Millions around the globe awoke to a great surprise on April 25, 1982. They opened their newspapers only to be greeted with full-page display ads brazenly proclaiming, "THE CHRIST IS NOW HERE."
>
> From Rome to Jerusalem, from Kuwait to Karachi and from New York to Los Angeles—in more than 20 major cities—newspaper readers blinked in shocked disbelief as they tried to digest this particular piece of "news" along with their breakfast.

The $500,000-plus ad campaign featured the following copy:

THE WORLD HAS HAD ENOUGH . . .
OF HUNGER, INJUSTICE, WAR.
IN ANSWER TO OUR CALL FOR HELP,
AS WORLD TEACHER FOR ALL HUMANITY,
THE CHRIST IS NOW HERE.[6]

So who was that ad talking about? Actually, it was talking about a man called Lord Maitreya. Maitreya is said to be the fifth reincarnation of Buddha, and New-Agers presented him as "The Christ." Texe Marrs in his book *Dark Secrets of the New Age* said, "Lord Maitreya, avatar and world teacher, is now claimed to be living in London, preparing himself for his eventual reign at the world's helm."[7]

The point I am making is that members of the New Age Movement are looking for a special person who will save them. What they fail to realize, however, is the basic dilemma of man— namely, that we have sinned against the living God and this means no mere human can save us, whether he is an Eastern guru, a Western religionist, or a secular humanist. Who, then, *can* save us? Only the Person of Isaiah's prophecy, only the Child who is born and the Son who is given, only Jesus Christ, the eternal Savior.

THIS PERSON IS JESUS CHRIST

According to Isaiah 9:6, Jesus Christ is qualified to be our Savior for two reasons. First, He is the unique man, unlike any other who has ever lived on Planet Earth; and second, He is the only God-man, the only One who alone can pay the price to free mankind from bondage to sin. Let's look at each of these in turn.

Jesus Christ Is the Unique Man

For a child will be born to us.

ISAIAH 9:6

The first thing we learn about this Child is that it will be a male child. The Savior of Isaiah's prophecy will be a man. The word for *child* in the Hebrew text is a masculine word; so the Child will be a boy. Now that immediately eliminates half of the population as potential candidates. The special Person who will come as the light to penetrate the darkness will not be a woman. As we come to the New Testament we discover that this Person is Jesus, a truly unique man.

Yet throughout the history of the church much has been made of Mary, the mother of Jesus, as the person of enlightenment and salvation. Even though the Bible doesn't exalt her in that way, the Church of Rome has proceeded to eclipse the glory of Christ by focusing on the glory of Mary. The attributes of her son are attributed to her—i.e., she was born sinless, she lived a sinless life, she ascended to heaven without experiencing the pain of death, and she is really the go-to person for the forgiveness of sins. Now let me be quick to say that Mary was a very special woman and greatly blessed of God, but nowhere in the Bible are these things said of her. Isaiah makes it clear: The special Person who will save us will not be a woman; He will be a man.

A second thing we learn from an earlier prophecy of Isaiah is that this Child will have a unique birth. All men are born of a woman, of course—even gurus. What makes Jesus stand out above every other person is that He was born of a *virgin* woman. This is what Isaiah tells us in 7:14: "Therefore the Lord Himself will give you a sign: Behold, a virgin will be with child and bear a son, and she will call His name Immanuel."

This is an unusual prophecy because it predicts something unprecedented in the course of human history. We all know that a virgin can't have a baby (without being artificially inseminated). It is impossible. If there is no male sperm, then fertilization doesn't take place. It's as simple as that. Yet Isaiah predicts that a virgin will conceive a child and give birth to a son. Now, that's amazing!

The word translated "virgin" here is from the Hebrew word *almah*, which can mean "virgin" or "young woman." The Revised Standard Version and the New English Version translate it as "young woman," but the motive behind that translation seems to be a liberal bias against the whole idea of a virgin giving birth to a child. There are strong reasons to favor translating the word *almah* as "virgin," however. Let me share a few of them with you.

(1) Every other use of the word *almah* in the Old Testament (used seven times[8]) is a definite reference to a virgin woman or unmarried maiden. The first time this word is used (in Genesis 24:43), Rebekah is called an *almah* before she even meets her future husband, Isaac. Earlier in the chapter (verse 16), her virginity is clarified: "And the girl was very beautiful, a virgin, and no man had had relations with her." How much clearer could it be? She is an *almah*—a virgin. Every other occurrence of *almah* in the Old Testament is like that. Clearly *almah* refers to a virgin woman, and Isaiah 7:14 is no exception.

(2) There is a Greek translation of the Old Testament called the Septuagint. It was translated by Hebrew scholars who were experts in the Hebrew language but also knew Greek. When they translated the word *almah* in Isaiah 7:14, they used the Greek word *parthenos*, which is the explicit word in the Greek language for a virgin woman.

(3) Finally, for those who have any remaining doubt,

Scripture itself gives us the key to interpreting Isaiah 7:14. The Gospel of Matthew (1:23), under the inspiration of the Holy Spirit, quotes Isaiah 7:14: "Behold, the virgin shall be with child . . ."; and Matthew also uses the word *parthenos*, the specific Greek word for virgin. There is no room for doubt that this is exactly what Isaiah meant when he said that this special Child would be born of a virgin woman.

Isaiah predicted that this Child would be born in a manner different from every other person in the world. He would be the Child of a virgin, and no other person in history can truthfully make that assertion. From the beginning of His earthly existence the Messiah would be singled out as a unique man: He was born of a virgin, led a sinless life, died a vicarious death, rose from the dead, and ascended into heaven. Who is like Him? What guru, what Maitreya, what celebrity, what political or religious leader is like Jesus?

Jesus Christ Is the Only God-man

For . . . a son will be given to us.
ISAIAH 9:6

There is something else that uniquely sets Christ apart and qualifies Him alone to be the Savior. Not only is Jesus Christ unique by being virgin-born—He is also unique by virtue of His nature: He alone is the God-man. It is intriguing to note Isaiah's language here. He tells us that the Child will be *born*, but that the Son will be *given*. Now this appears to be more than stylistic variation. The difference between being *born* and being *given* is crucial. Isaiah is saying that the Son will be given for the express reason that *the Son* was never born. As the eternal Son of God, He had always existed. According to Scripture He is the eternally existent second member of the triune Godhead.

Here again we are taken back to a previous chapter in Isaiah, where the name of the virgin-born Child would be Immanuel (7:14). Today this is a popular name for boys, especially in the Hispanic community where it is common to give children biblical names. But in Isaiah's day it was not common. The name in Isaiah 7:14 is actually a phrase describing the special nature of the Child. It is a compound of the Hebrew preposition *im* (meaning "with"), the plural suffix *anu* (meaning "us"), and the word *El* (the shortened form of the Hebrew word *Elohim*, meaning "God"). So Immanu-el literally means "God with us." This is why Matthew, when quoting this verse, says in a parenthetical explanation, "'THEY SHALL CALL HIS NAME IMMANUEL,' which translated means, 'GOD WITH US'" (1:23).

Now the ramifications of this are astounding. *Elohim* is the name used for God in the first verse of the Bible, which says, "In the beginning God [*Elohim*] created the heavens and the earth." So Isaiah was declaring that the virgin-born Child would be the God of the universe, the God who created the world! As a matter of confirmation Isaiah later says (in the verse we are considering) that the Child's name would be called "Mighty God" (Isa. 9:6).

You see, no mortal man can be the savior of the world because all mortals are corrupted by sin, and all mortals are limited by their finite humanity. The only One who can save us is the God-man. That is why Jesus is unique. He is the one and only God-man. No eastern guru, Lord Maitreya, or aspiring world ruler can legitimately make that claim. In the words of Isaiah, pluralism is doomed. There is only one Savior, and He is the unique Jesus!

THIS PERSON WILL SAVE US

There is a practical side to Israel's prophecy found in the little phrase "to us," which occurs twice in Isaiah 9:6: "For a child will be born *to us*, a son will be given *to us*" (emphasis added). This makes it all very personal—especially to Israel in the context, but also to all of God's people by way of application. Here is God's answer for our need. Here is real hope!

He Will Be a Real Man

> *For a child will be born to us.*
> Isaiah 9:6

When Isaiah said that the Child who would be born to the virgin would be Immanuel ("God with us," Isa. 7:14), he was not saying that there would be some spiritual epiphany or mystical presence of God that would suddenly emerge in the world. Nor was he speaking of an extraterrestrial superhuman descending upon our planet like E.T. in the Spielberg movie. He was telling us that an actual Child would be born of a virgin woman and that this Child would bring ultimate peace to the world (Isa. 9:7). He would be a real human being who would be able to adequately represent the human race in providing an adequate solution to the human dilemma.

You see, the message of the Bible is that human beings have sinned against God and have therefore come under the judgment of God's holy and just wrath. It's not an animal problem or an angel problem—it's a human problem. Now since humans are the ones guilty of this serious infraction of divine law, it is humans who must pay the penalty. That is why the writer to the Hebrews in the New Testament said, "For it is impossible for the blood of bulls and goats to take away sins" (Heb. 10:4). Neither can an angel atone for our guilt, because angels are not human, and this is a problem caused by humans. Therefore, any savior of mankind must also be a true human being.

But there is a serious problem that must be resolved. All

human beings are born of other human beings, and so all are a part of the condemned race. Every eastern guru, every Maitreya, every aspiring politician, every world ruler has been born of another human being and is consequently a part of the problem rather than a part of the solution. There is only one human being who doesn't fit this category, and that person is Jesus Christ. Why? Because He was born of a virgin—and that has never been true of any other man.

The fact that Jesus did not have an earthly father, although Joseph was his adoptive father and the source of all of his legal rights, meant that He did not inherit the problem of sin that permeates the human race (Rom. 5:12). Yet because He did have a human mother, He qualifies as a true human being. In other words, the virgin birth was the only means by which an adequate Savior could be produced for us. Jesus Christ is a true human being; but He is also a *sinless* human being. He is the only man in the history of the world of whom that can be said. Therefore, as the only unique man, He is our only possible Savior.

This is why no human ruler has ever been able to bring peace to the world. Many have tried, but none have succeeded. Hitler was a sinful man. So was Napoleon and Alexander the Great and Julius Caesar and Genghis Khan. Corruption cannot produce perfection, and no sinful human being can produce a righteous kingdom.

The Child of Isaiah's prophecy is the *one exception*, and He is the only hope for mankind. According to Matthew's Gospel (1:21-23; 4:12-17), Jesus Christ is the fulfillment of Isaiah's prophecy. He is a real person, and He had a real physical presence among us. Isaiah is careful to tell us that the "child will be born *to us*" (emphasis added). This means that He will be our human benefactor—our Savior.

He Will Be the True God

For . . . a son will be given to us.

ISAIAH 9:6

The Savior of mankind must not only be a true man—He must also actually be God. The task of atoning for man's sin and establishing a utopian kingdom where the pristine environment of the Garden of Eden is restored to Planet Earth is beyond any human endeavor. Only God could accomplish these things.

I am sure you have noticed that the gurus claim a divine nature, and New Agers aspire to personal deity. But when we take a closer look, it's a madness easily dispelled. The lies, the lust, the greed, the self-centeredness of those who are claiming such things belie their claims. Just look once, just cut through the religious rhetoric, just observe the pious charade. It is not God. It is simply man in all of his sinfulness wanting to be God—pretending to be God. The New Age ideology is not an enlightenment; it is an evasion of responsibility before the holiness of God. Man does not want to be accountable to God; so he pretends to be God. That way he can make up his own rules and liberate himself from eternal damnation.

Listen, there is no divine presence in our world apart from the Son who was given to us. When Jesus the Son of God was born of a virgin, He was born sinless, and He remained sinless throughout the course of His life. But the other thing to realize is that He was also Immanuel—"God with us." This was absolutely essential to His role as our Redeemer. Matthew made this connection when he described the birth of Christ:

"She will bear a Son; and you shall call His name Jesus, for it is He who will save His people from their sins."

Now all this took place that what was spoken by the Lord through the prophet might be fulfilled, saying,
"BEHOLD, THE VIRGIN SHALL BE WITH CHILD, AND SHALL BEAR A SON, AND THEY SHALL CALL HIS NAME IMMANUEL," *which translated means,* "GOD WITH US."

—MATTHEW 1:21-23

The name Jesus means "one who saves," and the idea according to Matthew is that He will save His people from their sins. Now "people" is a reference to a lot of people—in fact, all the people who will ever believe in Jesus as their Savior. So if Jesus is going to die for more than one person, He has to be infinite. You see, if He were only human, then after He had died for the first person, He'd be dead and of no use to anyone else in their sinful predicament. As a perfect, sinless substitute He could still only pay the penalty for one person's sin if He were merely one human being. The only way the Son could save more than one (in fact, millions) is if there were an infinite quality about Him. And only God is infinite.

That is why Matthew adds the prophecy of Isaiah 7:14 as an explanation of how Jesus could save His people (plural) from their sin. The only way is if He were what Isaiah said He would be—Immanuel, "God with us." In other words, the true Messiah-Savior of mankind has to be more than a mere man with good ideas and a winsome personality. He has to be God— or more specifically, He has to be the God-man.

Now Jesus *did* die for the sins of the world, and that is what the gospel message of the New Testament is all about. He accomplished the first stage of redemption—the liberation of the human soul from bondage to sin and eternal death by His sacrificial death on the cross. After rising from the dead, He then left this earth, promising to return. When He does return,

He will complete the redemption process by destroying those who perpetuate evil in the world and by lifting the curse upon creation. He will inaugurate the Kingdom Age and bring universal peace to the world. That is what the Bible says the Messiah will do. And that is what Jesus will do—because He is the God-man.

SO, WHY DON'T MORE PEOPLE BELIEVE IN JESUS?

Despite His uniqueness, many in our world dismiss Jesus as irrelevant. How can this be? Well, I can think of two possible reasons. One is indicated by 2 Corinthians 4:4, which says, "the god of this world has blinded the minds of the unbelieving, that they might not see the light of the gospel of the glory of Christ, who is the image of God." "The light of the gospel" is the same light that Isaiah described in Isaiah 9:2, but Scripture says that Satan has the ability to cause spiritual blindness in unbelievers. This is one reason people dismiss Jesus as irrelevant.

A second reason is what I would call insipid Christianity. Many people who reject Jesus are not rejecting Jesus per se. Rather, they are rejecting our portrayal of Jesus. As Christians, the way we represent Jesus in our daily lives is often inconsistent with the way He truly is. For instance, He is loving and righteous—and we are often perceived as being quite different than that. The difference that Jesus should make in our lives as the unique Christ is not seen by others; so they simply conclude that Jesus is irrelevant.

To a large extent we have turned Christianity into a religion. We dutifully go to church and speak our platitudes of praise and perform our rituals, but in the real world we live just like everybody else. We don't live the life of Christ, and so people do not see His uniqueness in us. This is why those who watch us simply see Christianity as another religion in the world.

I remember hearing a conversation years ago between two college students in which a Christian student was telling an unbeliever about Jesus. The unbelieving student said to the Christian, "Listen, if one-tenth of what you say about Jesus is true, then you ought to be ten times as excited." Wow! What an indictment on our apathy and casual approach to Jesus! No wonder people are not attracted to Him.

The truth of the matter is, though, that regardless of how we may misrepresent Him, Jesus is the unique Savior who is both a perfect man and the true God. The little Child in the Bethlehem manger grew to live a sinless life, taught us the truth about God, died on the cross for our sins, rose again from the dead, and is coming again in great power and glory as the King of kings and Lord of lords. There is no one like Him. And that's something to get excited about!

CONCLUSION

The uniqueness of Christ is seen in the fact that there has never been anyone else like Him. Many have claimed to be the ultimate savior of the world, but apart from Jesus Christ, none has been able to substantiate that claim. All great leaders have struggled with their own faults, and all would-be world conquerors have ended their lives in eventual failure and infamy. Only Jesus Christ has offered a solution to mankind's most pressing need—the problem of sin and pervasive selfishness—by dying on the cross as the full and final payment for man's guilt before God. Jesus alone has the qualifications of perfect humanity blended with absolute deity—the qualifications necessary to redeem and renovate our worn-out planet. Jesus is the Messiah, the Savior of the world.

So as we come to the end of this first chapter, let me ask you a question. Have *you* recognized the uniqueness of Christ to be your Savior? Only He can forgive your sins, and He alone can give you the hope of eternal life. According to the Bible, all He requires is that you put your faith in Him, trusting that His sacrificial death on the cross was for you too. Acknowledge your sinful condition, and reach out to the Savior. The Bible says that "WHOEVER WILL CALL UPON THE NAME OF THE LORD WILL BE SAVED" (Rom. 10:13). It's as simple, and at the same time as profound, as that.

2

More Than a Politician

The Ultimate Ruler of the New World

. . . And the government will rest on his shoulder . . .
ISAIAH 9:6, KJV

Do you ever feel like you are bearing the weight of the world on your shoulders? Perhaps things have gone wrong, something has broken down, or plans have been interrupted or delayed. A myriad of problems lay clustered around your feet. Unfortunately, you seem to be the person to whom everyone is looking to "fix it." Or maybe it's the sheer burden of having too much to do. You literally wish that you were a dozen people, all of whom had the strength of Samson and the wisdom of Solomon. Perhaps then you could make at least a dent in the problem.

Our world is filled with scenarios like that. Now some people handle overload better than others, but everyone sometimes faces a task that exceeds his or her limitations. Then it is no longer a challenge—it becomes a *burden*. That's the picture of Atlas, with the world perched on his shoulder.

Atlas was a giant, according to the mythical tale, the son of Titan Iapetus and a nymph by the name of Clymene. This giant was the king of Mauritania in northwest Africa near the Strait of Gibraltar. Numerous legends surround the story of Atlas, one of which says that he was condemned to hold up the earth with his head and hands as a penalty for aiding the Titans against Zeus, the father of the gods. Thus holding the world on his shoulders was not an honor or exhibition of strength for Atlas. It was a punishment.

In another of the legends, a son of Zeus named Perseus once came to the entrance of the Mediterranean Sea where the giant Atlas lived. The land was rich with flocks and herds, and Atlas was proud of his garden of the Hesperides, where he had a tree of golden apples. Now Atlas had been warned by an oracle that one day a son of Zeus would come and steal his golden apples. So when Perseus presented himself as the son of Zeus and asked for rest and hospitality, Atlas not only refused him but used violence to drive him from the land. In response, Perseus took out of his pouch the gorgon's head, whose face would turn anyone to stone who looked upon it. As fate would have it, Atlas looked and was changed into a mountain. His beard and hair became trees, his bones became rock, and upon his shoulders rested the weight of the world and the sky with all of its stars. Today Mount Atlas in Africa can still be seen guarding the entrance to the Mediterranean Sea just across from Gibraltar.

Actually, the Bible also presents Jesus Christ as holding the world upon His shoulder but in a way that contrasts strikingly with classic mythology. In the mythological story, Atlas is saddled with an unwanted burden: The world, the stars, and the heavens are placed upon him as a punishment for not cooperating with

Zeus. The Bible, on the other hand, presents the Messiah with the world upon His shoulder not as a burden but rather as an anticipated reward for accomplishing God's purpose in the world. Isaiah's prophecy says, "For unto us a child is born, unto us a son is given (KJV)," and then it goes on to say, "and the government shall be upon his shoulder" (Isaiah 9:6, KJV).

It is this phrase, "and the government shall be upon his shoulder," that is the subject of this chapter. Isaiah is referring to the government of God as it will one day be manifest on the earth, and he is saying that this special Child will be the ruler of that government. The Child who will be born, the Son who will be given, is the long-awaited global ruler who will govern the world from the throne of David. Isaiah continues in the next verse, "There will be no end to the increase of *His* government or of peace, on the throne of David and over his kingdom, to establish it and to uphold it with justice and righteousness from then on and forevermore. The zeal of the LORD of hosts will accomplish this" (Isa. 9:7).

In the New Testament this prophecy is applied to Jesus Christ. When the angel made his announcement to Mary concerning the Child who would be born to her, he said, "And behold, you will conceive in your womb, and bear a son, and you shall name Him Jesus. He will be great, and will be called the Son of the Most High; and the Lord God will give Him the throne of His father David; and He will reign over the house of Jacob forever; and His kingdom will have no end" (Luke 1:31-33). Now, those are the thoughts gleaned from Isaiah's prophecy, and Luke applies them to Jesus Christ, the Child born to the virgin Mary. In short, Jesus is the Child of Isaiah's prophecy upon whose shoulder will be placed the government of the world. So let's consider this statement by Isaiah by looking at each of the words in this captivating phrase.

THERE IS ONLY ONE RIGHTEOUS GOVERNMENT

Only one government is indeed righteous—the government of God. That is the message of the Bible. The word "government" in Isaiah's text is a Hebrew word that means dominion or lordship. It comes from a root verb that carries the idea "to prevail" or "to have power." This word is used two times by Isaiah— once in verse 6 where we read, "and the *government* shall be upon his shoulder," and again in verse 7, which says, "there shall be no end" of the "increase of *government* and peace" (KJV, emphasis mine).

Now the basic thrust of this word is not so much toward the administrative side of government, the organizational side, in the sense that He will be able to run the government well (which of course He can, and will). Rather, the idea behind this word is that of prevailing over others, having dominion and exercising power and lordship. In other words, when Jesus Christ returns to set up the government of God on the earth, no opposition will be able to resist His overwhelming power and authority. Scripture says that He will simply speak and His enemies will be decimated (Rev. 19:11-16).

Another observation here is that the article "the" is used with this word, so it is "*the* government" (v. 6). Isaiah is drawing attention to a specific government spoken of in the Word of God when the Messiah (the Anointed One) will come and rule upon the earth. This government is "*the* government," and it will prevail over all the others. It will have complete dominion, and it will exercise power and lordship over the entire globe. It is this government that is predicted by all of the prophets in the Bible.

For instance, the great prophecy given in Psalm 2 begins with a rebellion of the leaders of the earth against the Lord and against His Anointed One: "Let us break their bands asunder, and cast away their cords from us," they boastingly cry (v. 3,

KJV). Then God merely laughs at their stupidity and speaks to them in His wrath, causing great derision in their ranks (vv. 4-5). Finally God says,

> 6 *Yet have I set my king upon my holy hill of Zion. 7 . . . the* LORD *hath said unto me, Thou art my Son; this day have I begotten thee. 8 Ask of me, and I shall give thee the heathen for thine inheritance, and the uttermost parts of the earth for thy possession. 9 Thou shalt break them with a rod of iron; thou shalt dash them in pieces like a potter's vessel.*
>
> —vv. 6-9, KJV

Then at the end of the Psalm a message is given to the rulers of the earth: "Kiss the Son, lest he be angry . . . when his wrath is kindled but a little. Blessed *are* all they that put their trust in him" (v. 12, KJV). Wow! What a prediction, and what a warning! You see, it is *that Son* and His government to which Isaiah is referring. There is only one righteous government, and that is the government of the Son of God.

Man's Government Tends Toward Corruption

A college degree in history is not necessary to realize that the governments of men tend toward corruption. A survey of history will confirm that this is the way it has always been. Even great empires (the Roman Empire, the British Empire, etc.) lost their strength more as a result of internal decay than from any superior external force. The reason, according to the Bible, is that man is sinful, and therefore everything that humans do is tainted with the corrupting influence of their sinful nature.

Even nations that begin well have this inherent weakness. In the context of Isaiah's prophecy we are confronted with the turmoil of national governments. In Chapter 1 of this book we noted that civil war had divided the nation of Israel into a northern kingdom (Ephraim) and a southern kingdom (Judah). The northern kingdom had gone through a terrible crisis of government as a result of having done evil in the sight of the Lord. Consequently, God allowed another godless government, the Assyrians, to invade the land and take the people captive.

Now as Isaiah was writing his prophecy, the people of Judah were acting just like their northern brethren, and they were in danger as well. Their government had become corrupt, and God was threatening to allow Babylon, another heathen government, to take them into captivity. It was all a mad cycle of corruption, deterioration, and demise. This was the setting of Isaiah's prophecy, and he was speaking in the midst of impending doom caused by the corruption of human government.

Listen, if history teaches us anything, it teaches us that man's government tends toward corruption. A particular government may begin with noble intentions and may continue for a time with high ideals; but eventually it will succumb to its sinful nature, and in the process it will sow the seeds of its own demise.

This reminds me of the story of the senior citizen who was trying to impress his grandson. With an air of pride he said to the child, "You know, I have the body of a twenty-year-old." To which the grandson replied, "Grandpa, I think you'd better give it back. You're getting it all wrinkled." Well, life tends to deteriorate, doesn't it? And governments do the same. They may think they have the body of a twenty-year-old, as it were, but they're getting it all wrinkled.

This propensity of human government toward self-destruction is graphically illustrated in The American Adventure at Disney's EPCOT Center. Upon entering the American Pavilion at the top of the World Showcase Lagoon, guests are ushered into a large theater to be entertained with a tremendous display of American history. The glory of our nation's beginnings and the struggles of the American people through the wars that threatened to destroy the nation are graphically portrayed. Viewers can only be impressed by the way the American people pulled together in the face of great adversity and the demonstration of unity that made them strong.

At that point in the program a dramatic scene unfolds in which Samuel Clemens (Mark Twain) is talking with Benjamin Franklin about the future of America in light of its glorious past. In their discussion Samuel Clemens quotes John Steinbeck, the great contemporary American author who stressed the idea that no nation can withstand the eroding effects of success and prosperity. You see, Steinbeck saw the seeds of the demise of our American way of life in the very thing of which we boast: our success and prosperity.[1] In fact, that is the very thing today that is undermining the entire fabric of our society. The deterioration and the corruption we observe in our land today is strikingly similar to what has happened over the centuries to every other prosperous government. I guess the saying is true that those who don't learn from history are destined to repeat it.

Actually, the basic problem with government is not in the administering of the affairs of a society, though there is potential for abuse in this area as well. Rather, the real problem stems from the fact that government represents power. It is the means by which one person or a group of people rules over others, and as Lord Acton wrote, "Power tends to corrupt, and absolute power corrupts absolutely."[2] That lust for power has been the temptation for all rulers over the years, and more than anything else, it has been the culprit at the core of corruption in human government.

This downward spiral toward corruption is illustrated in George Orwell's insightful book *Animal Farm*, first published in

1945.[3] In this satirical allegory on collectivism (or Communism), the animals on Farmer Jones's farm stage a revolution. As with all revolutions, there are leaders, and there are followers. In this case the pigs became the leaders since they were, through no fault of their own, a little smarter than the others. One of their first official acts was to draft a statement of seven principles, which they then painted on the back wall of the barn for all to see. These principles became the basis of the New Order, whose purpose was to protect the animals from any future injustice or infringement of their rights. The principles included noble pronouncements such as "No animal shall drink alcohol" and "No animal shall sleep in a bed" and "No animal shall kill any other animal." But the greatest and wisest of these was the last, which said, "All animals are equal."[4]

Well, as the months became years, things did not turn out quite the way the workers had expected. They were working twice as hard, but they were eating half as well as when they were exploited by Farmer Jones—all of them, that is, except the ruling pigs, who were now drinking Farmer Jones's ale and were sleeping in his bed. When the troubled workers tried to figure out why the revolution had turned out so poorly, they went to see whether something in the seven principles prohibited this kind of injustice. To their surprise, as they began reading the principles, they noticed slight changes in the wording. Now they read, "No animal shall drink alcohol *to excess*,"[5] "No animal shall sleep in a bed *with sheets*,"[6] "No animal shall kill any other animal *without just cause*."[7] But by far the worst shock of all came much later when the poor creatures turned with hope to the seventh principle, which now declared, "ALL ANIMALS ARE EQUAL BUT SOME ANIMALS ARE MORE EQUAL THAN OTHERS."[8]

George Orwell certainly understood the nature of collectivism as a system of government. Yet what he described has always been the nature of all human government because of the ultimate selfishness of the human heart. All who are currently putting their hope in a New World Order or some other governmental concept such as the United Nations world court would do well to go to the back of the barn and ponder Orwell's words. Fundamental to the laws of man's depravity is the unalterable principle that man's government tends toward corruption.

God's Government Leads to Satisfaction

The good news is that there is a government that will not let people down but will bring about the very conditions that lead to peace and long-lasting satisfaction—and that is the government of God. It is this government that is spoken of in Isaiah 9:6 when Isaiah says, "And the *government* will rest on His shoulder" (emphasis added). This is the government that will be brought about by the Child who "will be born" and the Son who "will be given."

The nature of this government is described by Isaiah in the very next verse (7) when he goes on to say,

> *There will be no end to the increase of His government or of peace, on the throne of David and over his kingdom, to establish it and to uphold it with justice and righteousness from then on and forevermore. The zeal of the* LORD *of hosts will accomplish this.*

Notice what Isaiah says about this government. He says that "there will be no end to . . . peace" and that the rule of this government will be upheld "with justice and righteousness." Peace, justice, and righteousness! These are the very things we long for in our hearts. We all want peace without end, and who doesn't wish for the kind of justice that is fair to all? Genuine righteousness, right prevailing over wrong and good triumphing over evil, is the universal dream of humanity. Yet sadly, these are the very things that are so elusive in our troubled world.

How, then, will these things ever come about? Well, at the end of verse 7 Isaiah tells us how: "The zeal of the LORD of hosts will accomplish this." Man has never been able to sustain this kind of just and righteous government—only God can produce it. In this prophecy of Isaiah, God will bring it about through the special virgin-born Child who is the Son of God. For "the government shall be upon his shoulder" (Isaiah 9:6, KJV).

You see, the Hebrew prophets, including Isaiah, did speak of a new world order on earth under Messiah's rule. They wrote of a Kingdom of perfect peace that was void of corruption and pollution, with sickness and death rare, where the earth is then a paradise. Isaiah, for instance, in chapter 11 gives us a comprehensive statement about the nature of Messiah's future reign:

> *4 But with righteousness He will judge the poor, and decide with fairness for the afflicted of the earth; and He will strike the earth with the rod of His mouth, and with the breath of His lips He will slay the wicked. 5 Also righteousness will be the belt about His loins, and faithfulness the belt about His waist. 6 And the wolf will dwell with the lamb, and the leopard will lie down with the kid, and the calf and the young lion and the fatling together; and a little boy will lead them. 7 Also the cow and the bear graze; their young will lie down together; and the lion will eat straw like the ox. 8 And the nursing child will play by the hole of the cobra, and the weaned child will put his hand on the viper's den. 9 They will not hurt or destroy in all My holy mountain, for the earth will be full of the knowledge of the LORD as the waters cover*

*the sea. **10** Then it will come about in that day that the nations will resort to the root of Jesse, who will stand as a signal for the peoples; and His resting place will be glorious.*

—vv. 4-10

Isn't that a wonderful description of our utopian dream? What a contrast to the day in which we live and to the trends we are currently seeing in our world! What a relief it will be when the government finally rests upon the shoulder of the Anointed One of God. We again read of this Kingdom in Psalm 85:10: "Mercy and truth are met together; righteousness and peace have kissed *each other*" (KJV). What a glorious hope!

So take heart. Isaiah is telling us that a new age is coming; a new world order is in the plan of God for our future. The prophet is saying that a universal government of liberty and justice for all has been promised to us by God. But he is also saying that this new reality is not the global hope of humanism. The government of God will come through His only begotten Son— the Child who was born, the Son who was given. This Person is Jesus Christ, for He alone is the prophesied God-man who was born of a virgin; and He alone is qualified, by virtue of His sacrificial death on the cross for our redemption, to bring the righteous government of God to pass upon the earth.

What Does All of This Mean Now?

Let's take a moment to apply this truth to our current circumstances. A Kingdom Age may be the promise of God for the future of the world, but right now that seems a long way off. What we face in the here and now is a lack of peace in our world; and justice and righteousness are increasingly rare. It's all very troubling. So how does hope in a future kingdom help us *now*?

First of all, we need to understand that the Kingdom of God on earth is not just for some future generation. It is the living hope of every believer in Jesus Christ that one day we will live and reign with Him on the earth. Those who have died will be resurrected, so that no child of God will miss out on this climactic age on earth following our Lord's return. It is a *real* hope of living in *real* peace, and it includes all of us who are true believers.

On the campus of Wheaton College in Wheaton, Illinois, there is a monument-type of sign on the southwest lawn identifying the college. On that sign are etched the words, "For Christ and His Kingdom." That should be the heartbeat of every Christian who lives and works in the world—to advance the cause of Christ by preparing for His Kingdom. What a cause! Some people work tirelessly for a political campaign in order to secure the establishment of their particular brand of government. We as Christians should exhibit that same dedicated commitment in anticipation of the government of Jesus Christ. Persuading others to become followers of our Lord is the principal means by which believers in every generation can advance the Kingdom of Christ.

A second benefit is to realize that there is a spiritual dimension to the Kingdom that affects us now. When any person receives Jesus Christ as his or her personal Savior, Christ actually comes to live within that person's life by means of the Holy Spirit (1 Cor. 6:19; Gal. 2:20; Col. 1:27). What that means is that the qualities of Christ can be experienced in the everyday life of the believer. In other words, when Christ rules in the human heart, He brings about substantially the same results as when He will rule in His government over the earth.

Take a moment to ponder that wonderful truth; it's incredible! Listen, if Jesus Christ is *your* Savior, and you are submitting to His rule in *your* life, then *you* will experience peace. It's as simple as that. To the extent that you don't experience peace, you can assume that there are areas in your life that are not under His control. In the same way, when Christ is Lord of your life, there will be within you a great desire to be fair and just with others. You will want to act righteously, to see right triumph over wrong in all your affairs. You see, wherever Jesus is governor, these qualities of life will be the fruits of His governance. The peace, justice, and righteousness of Christ can be yours in the here and now.

Think of what it would do for your marriage or your family life if Jesus were truly the governor of your home. The problem is that we try to govern our own affairs, and *our* government tends toward corruption in the same way as political governments do. The reason, of course, is that we are innately selfish, and that tends to ruin everything we touch. There is an antidote for all of our troubles, though: We must recognize that in order for things to go well, the government must be upon *His* shoulders. Only Jesus can turn the core of your being and the heart and soul of your marriage, family, and workplace from a sinful wilderness into a garden paradise. He is particularly good at doing that—but we must understand that *only* He can do it!

As a pastor for many years, I have seen this simple truth transform bad situations into beautiful experiences. It is the ultimate secret in counseling needy people: Lead them to Jesus, guide them to a trusting relationship with Him, and then simply step back and watch Him perform the miracle of life as He leads them to discover the joy of abundant living. After forty years of ministry I am more convinced than ever that Jesus Christ is the answer—to everything!

Let me share an example from the corporate experience of

church life. A number of years ago I was invited to become the interim pastor of a historically vibrant church. This church had just come through a very difficult time that threatened to tear it apart. The former pastor had been fired amidst allegations of divisiveness and moral indiscretion, and factions had developed, polarizing the congregation around the issues. Business meetings turned into arguments, and people were becoming angry with one another. It was a mirror image of the problems we see today in the turmoil of the world.

The situation was difficult, but I knew the answer to their problem. These people needed to get their eyes off themselves and begin focusing their hearts on Jesus Christ. So I accepted their invitation to be interim pastor and began preaching messages that exalted the preeminence of Christ. I helped the leadership to understand how they could know the mind of Christ in the affairs of the church. Slowly the healing began to take place; individuals began to confess their selfishness, and alienated parties sought reconciliation. Peace, justice, and righteousness began to prevail in the ministry once again, and the beauty of Christ was emerging from the ashes of turmoil.

A year later this church called a wonderful man of God to be their pastor; and at his welcoming celebration they also presented me with something very special. That evening they gave me a framed "Doctor's Degree" that said in part, "in recognition of service to the Lord on our behalf, we the church family . . . hereby confer upon Daniel Robert Hayden, the honorary degree of Doctor of Church Medicine." Now I'm not sure if anyone else has received that kind of degree, but it was certainly an honor that I will never forget. I have several degrees from college and seminaries, but this "Doctor of Church Medicine" degree brings joy to my heart above all the others, for it is an expression of appreciation from a congregation for what Christ did in their church. It was not me—I didn't heal their church. I simply took them to Jesus, and *He* healed them.

That, then, is the point. The government of men leads to corruption and ruin; but the government of Christ produces health, peace, and prosperity. Wherever Christ is honored and obeyed, there will be healing and hope; but wherever He is ignored or marginalized, frustration and demise will ultimately result. Jesus Christ is everything, and for any governance (marriage, family, church, community) to be successful, the government must rest upon His shoulder.

THERE IS ONLY ONE ADEQUATE RULER

We should note a couple of things regarding the phrase, "shall be upon his shoulder" (Isaiah 9:6, KJV). Before we are told who He is through His name in the rest of the verse, we are introduced to what He does: *He is the strength of the government of God.*

The Ruler Is the Son of God

" . . . *shall be upon his shoulder" (KJV).*

The Person who has the government on His shoulder is the Child who was born, the Son who was given. Those phrases are the antecedent (they come before) to the pronoun "his" in this verse; this means that "his" is a reference to those phrases. Remember, we have already seen that Jesus Christ is the fulfillment of this prophecy (Luke 1:31-33). The angel's explanation to Mary concerning what was happening to her with the virgin-conceived Child in her womb was, "therefore . . . that holy thing which shall be born of thee shall be called the Son of God" (Luke 1:35, KJV). It is clear, then, that the One on whose shoulder the government rests is the Son of God.

Jesus, the Son of God, will rule over the government of God

in this world. He is the strength of the government of God. No Indian guru or Lord Maitreya (fifth generation of Buddha) will have the ability or authority to accomplish God's purposes on the earth. No aspiring politician or blueblood monarch will emerge as the ultimate ruler. It is only the Son of God who can bring a lasting government of peace, justice, and righteousness to our beleaguered planet. These are things that only God can produce, and that is why Isaiah said, "The zeal of the LORD of hosts will accomplish this" (9:7). Jesus Christ is the only adequate ruler because He is the Son of God. The government will rest upon *His* shoulder.

This Ruler Has Divine Ability

"*. . . shall be upon his shoulder*" *(KJV).*

Because this ruler is the Son of God, He is able to do what needs to be done. He has divine ability. The word *shoulder* is a Hebrew word that carries the idea of strength and stability. It is the word for the strong upper part of the back and neck—or the shoulder. This is the picture of Atlas with the world resting on his shoulder, indicating his ability to uphold and sustain the affairs of the world.

Our world is looking for a powerful ruler who is strong in character and who has the wisdom and ability to solve the world's ills. The problem is that man's wisdom and strength are finite. Every man and woman, including the great rulers of the world, is limited in what he or she can do. That has always been the way it is, and the future can be no different.

I am sure you have noticed how politicians promise the sky but deliver considerably less. When they get into office they often use their power and influence to further their own ends. Congress invariably makes its decisions based on political advantage, which is why no one wants to take on a difficult issue during an election year. A number of years ago one of the space shuttle missions included a scientific experiment that required the use of jellyfish and rats, and I remember, as the shuttle lifted off and ascended into the sky, someone quipped, "There goes the Congress." It was a pathetically humorous depiction of the public's general perception of their elected officials.

You see, what we truly need is a strong shoulder on which to lean. We need a reliable leader who truly has the interests of the people at heart. We need superhuman strength to overcome the problems around us. What we truly need is the strength of Almighty God and the wisdom of the Creator. And who is that? Only Jesus—the omnipotent, omniscient Son of God. He's the only adequate ruler because He's the only One who has divine ability.

This Ruler Will Surely Come

" . . . *shall be upon his shoulder*" *(KJV)*.

Perhaps all of this sounds as if it is pie-in-the-sky dreaming— a fable drawn from the stories of Aesop. Well, it is not! This magnificent prophecy of Isaiah has all of the authority of the Word of God. This is a truth that is as sure as the sun. As the darkness and clouds are cleared away, the sun is still there. In every rotation of the earth, day after day, it is always there. What the Lord has spoken *shall be*!

Some very interesting things about this verb, "shall be," enhance the certainty of this phrase. First of all, it is a verb of simple reality. It is not complicated by extraneous ideas or a compound root structure. There is nothing fancy or esoteric about its meaning. It is straightforward and clear: This is what "shall be."

Second, in the original language it is the first word in the phrase. Literally the text says, *"and shall be* the government upon his shoulder." Now, it is not unusual for a Hebrew phrase to begin with the verb, but it *does* lend a certain importance to the action of the verb by stressing the fact that this government of divine ability *shall be.*

And third, there is a grammatical structure associated with this verb that emphasizes the certainty of the event. The word "and" is attached as a prefix to this word, and when this occurs in a context of consecutive narrative, the action of the verb changes to its alternate. So instead of incomplete action (future tense: "shall be"), the verb becomes completed action (present tense: "is"). In actuality, the phrase should read, " . . . and the government *is* upon his shoulder." Now some may think this is stretching or belaboring a grammatical point; but there is great impact in realizing that this phrase is written as an already established fact. It becomes not just a statement of future hope ("this is what shall be"), but a record of already conceived reality. You see, in the economy of God there is no time. And what "shall be" *is*—if God has decreed it. The establishment of the Kingdom of God on earth by the Son of God, although it is yet to happen in the realm of time, is viewed as an already accomplished historical event in the mind of God.

CONCLUSION

What Isaiah is giving us in this marvelous verse is a wonderful blend of the first and second advents of Christ. An advent is a coming, and with Jesus Christ there are two comings. The first advent is indicated by the statements "a child will be born" and "a son will be given." Here the focus is on redemption for mankind through the birth of Jesus in Bethlehem. The second advent is emphasized in the next statement, "and the government shall be upon his shoulder" (KJV). This is a reference to the

Second Coming of Christ, where He will present Himself as the King of kings to reign upon the earth.

Listen, when Jesus comes again, He will change the course of this world forever! Isaiah tells us in verse 7, "Of the increase of *his* government and peace *there shall be* no end" (KJV). The presence of Jesus will make all the difference in the world! And all who love and trust Him will share in the joys of the Kingdom Age forever.

But I would remind you that the presence of Jesus Christ will not only change the course of history as far as the future is concerned—He is also available in the here and now to change the course of *your* life. When you receive Him as your Savior and acknowledge His governance over every area of your life, He will make all the difference in the world! He will change your marriage and family life into a joyful experience of kingdom living, He will bring peace into your heart in the workplace or community, and He is certainly able to transform your church by revolutionizing the dynamics of corporate fellowship. It is the exaltation and preeminence of Jesus that makes the difference.

My hope, as you read this book, is that you will reflect upon the fact that the Child who was born, the Son who was given, is the Glorious Ruler upon whose shoulder is the government of God. Acknowledge His lordship, and submit to His authority in every area of life. It is the only means of experiencing true peace and lasting fulfillment.

THAT'S AN UNUSUAL NAME

The Special Names That Set Him Apart

"And His name will be called . . ."
ISAIAH 9:6

A person's name is an important part of his or her identity. People like to be referred to by their names. I'm a name-tag reader; so when I go through a checkout counter or engage a waitress in a restaurant, I will invariably address the person by name. Occasionally the response is humorous: "How do you know me?" Then the person remembers that she's wearing a name-tag, and we both laugh at the situation. But I've also noticed that it warms the encounter and elevates it from mere business to a friendly interaction. People like it when you call them by name.

I have a brother who understands the significance of names in business. For many years he was a business entrepreneur, and now he is a successful business analyst and corporate coach. His customers and acquaintances would often refer to him by his last name, Hayden, as if it were a first name. Now you probably know that the name Hayden is an increasingly popular first name (for example, Hayden Fry, the former football head coach at Iowa). Well, my brother's first name was David, but he decided to legally change his name to Hayden Hayden, since that's what people were calling him anyway. It was a clever business decision. Now everyone who meets him for the first time is impressed by his name, and his business card evokes smiles of affirmation. Hayden Hayden is so unique, it's easy to remember.

When we name our children, we give a lot of thought to what we will call them. Sometimes it's the meaning of a name that impresses us, and other times we just like the sound of a particular name, or we choose a name of a relative or favorite friend. When I was born, my parents wanted to name me after my father, but they didn't want a "junior." So they simply turned the name around. My father's name was Robert Daniel; so they named me Daniel Robert. Then when my wife and I had a son, we continued the tradition and named him Robert Daniel, after his grandfather. Now my son has a son—and guess what he is named? No, my son is too smart for that. He and his wife named their first son Josiah. The curse of the flip-flopping of names is now over. Whew!

In another sense, names often reflect *who a person is* by defining some characteristic of life. For instance, Native Americans would often give names to their people in this way—Red Cloud, Sitting Bull, Crazy Horse, and so on. When our son played sports during his high school and college years, his friends nicknamed him Weasel. I thought that was pretty cool. After all, a weasel is a clever little animal and very tenacious. It was a great name for an athlete. Then one day I asked his best friend why they nicknamed our son Weasel. "Oh," he said, "that's simple. He has asthma, and he wheezes." How's that for a letdown!

What's in a name? Actually, names are important, and that

is especially true in the Bible because the meaning of names often reflects some characteristic of the person's life. As we have noticed, in Isaiah 7:14, for example, we read, "Behold, a virgin will be with child and bear a son, and she will call His name Immanuel." Matthew in his Gospel tells us that Immanuel means "God with us" (Matt. 1:23). Now this is very significant with regard to who Jesus is. The Bible tells us that Jesus is no ordinary man—He really is "God with us." So you see, the name Immanuel is a significant name when applied to Jesus.

In the remainder of this book we are going to look at some of the names given to Jesus. In Isaiah 9:6 Isaiah reveals four special names for Christ, and we will look at each one of them in turn: Wonderful Counselor, Mighty God, Everlasting Father, and Prince of Peace. Each of these names is incredibly significant with regard to who Jesus is and what He did and will do. But before we do that, I would like for us to consider the phrase that introduces those designations: "And His name will be called . . ."

OBSERVATIONS ON HIS NAME
"And His name will be called . . ."

Let me share four observations on this phrase in Isaiah 9:6 that will help us understand the way the Bible uses names for this special Son in Isaiah's prophecy. We have already seen that the Child-Son spoken of by Isaiah is Jesus Christ, the Child who was born to the virgin Mary in Bethlehem; so the names are descriptive of Jesus. However:

1. Jesus Christ Was Never Specifically Called by These Names

First of all, we need to notice that Jesus was never specifically called Wonderful Counselor, Mighty God, Everlasting Father, or

Prince of Peace. Does this mean that He did not fulfill this prophecy? No, not at all! Although Jesus was never called by these names, He is certainly deserving of them; and furthermore, they are descriptive of who He is. The Child born in Bethlehem was named Jesus, and later when He began His ministry He was called by other names such as Rabbi, Christ, and Lord. Yet He was a Wonderful Counselor to people who came to Him. He demonstrated the power of Mighty God in his special miracles and healings. He taught that He was one with the Everlasting Father and that He would one day return to earth as the Prince of Peace. Yes, He was all of these things, and it would be a mistake to think that these designations do not apply to Him.

W. A. Criswell, for many years the beloved pastor of the First Baptist Church of Dallas, Texas, and a wonderful preacher, on one occasion reflected on the names of Christ in the Bible from both the Old and New Testaments. In that study he mentioned that there are 256 different names for Christ in the Bible, all of which are expressions of the "infinite virtue and worth of His marvelous life."[1] Think of it—256 different names! That's a lot of names, and yet Jesus was actually called by very few of them.

Consider the ways we normally refer to our Lord. We call Him *Lord*, which is from the Greek word *kurios* and the Old Testament Hebrew word *adonai*. In both languages it means "one who is master" and was used for people in authority. We also call Him *Jesus*, because that was the official name given to Him by Joseph at His birth (Matt. 1:20-25). It was the angel Gabriel who, as a messenger from heaven, told Joseph to give the Child that name because it meant "He will save" (v. 21; cf. Luke 1:26-31). Gabriel explained that the reason for naming Him Jesus was that He would "save His people from their sins" (Matt. 1:21). Then too, we call Him *Christ*, which some people seem to think is His last name—Jesus Christ. Actually, Christ is a name that means "Anointed One" and comes from the Greek word *chrio*, which means "to anoint." The corresponding Hebrew word in the Old Testament is *masiaḥ*, from which we get the word *Messiah*, "the Anointed One." And so we call Him the *Lord Jesus Christ*—the One who is Master, who will save His people from their sins, and who is the Anointed One of God. Each designation of His name, you see, carries great meaning!

All of the other names for Christ in the Scriptures are like that too. They are meaningful designations of who He is and what He does. So what we have in Isaiah 9:6 are four couplets that are descriptive designations of who He is and that point prophetically to Him as the divinely anointed Messiah. This is the point made by Merrill F. Unger in his two-volume commentary on the Old Testament when he says, "His name is a Hebrew idiom, which means that He would not actually bear those names, but that He would deserve them"; they would be "descriptive designations of His person and work."[2]

Consider for a moment how Jesus is described in the Gospels in the light of Isaiah's four couplet names. The first is *Wonderful Counselor*. This name is certainly appropriate as applied to Christ. In John 14, for instance, Jesus told His disciples that He was going away, but that when He did He would send them "another Helper" (v. 16), referring to the work of the Holy Spirit. This word "Helper" is the Greek word *parakletos*, which essentially means "one called alongside" for the purpose of helping. The English word used by the King James Version is "Comforter," which certainly has an application in the context of John 14. But the disciples needed more than comfort at that point; they needed guidance. John uses this same Greek word *parakletos* in 1 John 2:1, and there it is translated "Advocate"— one who comes alongside to help in time of crisis. An advocate is a lawyer—someone who gives counsel. Now that's what Jesus was saying in John 14. Another "Helper" or "Comforter" meant another Counselor just like Him. The Holy Spirit would guide them just like Jesus had done. Can there be any question but that Jesus is a "Wonderful Counselor"? Indeed, there is no counselor who is His equal.

What about *Mighty God*? Well, for starters, John's whole Gospel is dedicated to demonstrating that "Jesus is the Christ, the Son of God" (John 20:31). The miracles, as well as the discourses, of Christ are undeniable proof that Jesus is indeed God among us. At the end of the Gospel of John there is an interesting story that illustrates this point that John is making. After Jesus had risen from the dead, He made two appearances to His disciples in the Upper Room. Thomas wasn't there the first time, and being skeptical by nature, he doubted the report that Jesus was really alive. A week later Jesus appeared again, and this time He showed Thomas the nail-prints in His hands and feet, as well as the wound in His side. This inherent skeptic then fell on his face and cried, "My Lord and my God!" (John 20:28). John is making the point that the evidence is so strong that even the most ardent critic is compelled to believe that Jesus is indeed "Mighty God."

Eternal Father or *Everlasting Father* (KJV) can be a somewhat misleading rendering of the Hebrew text, as if the Son were in some way also the Father. But that is not what the Hebrew is saying at all, as I will endeavor to show in more detail in Chapter 6. What the Hebrew actually says is, "*Father of Eternity.*" In other words, Scripture is indicating that the Child of Isaiah's prophecy is the source of eternal life for those who place their trust in Him. Now it is true that Jesus is one with the Father, as Jesus Himself said in John 10:30 (cf. John 14:7-9); but that is not the idea behind the name *Father of Eternity*. Rather, it is the point Jesus consistently made—that He was the doorway to heaven, the only way for sinful people to obtain eternal life (John 10:9; 11:25-26; 14:6). Therefore, *Father of Eternity* is also an apt designation for who Jesus is.

And is Jesus the *Prince of Peace*? Clearly the answer is, yes! When the angels announced the birth of Christ to the shepherds, they went on to say, "on earth peace, goodwill toward men!" (Luke 2:14, NKJV). That is exactly what Isaiah had predicted in his prophecy concerning the Child who would be born (Isa. 9:6-7). Then, just prior to Jesus' crucifixion, Jesus told His disciples, "Peace I leave with you; My peace I give to you; not as the world gives, do I give to you" (John 14:27). The peace of Jesus surpasses any peace the world could ever know. He is the only One with divine resources to give us the peace of God. Is He the *Prince of Peace*? Of course He is!

Every one of these designations by Isaiah is appropriate to our Lord, for they describe who He really is. He certainly does fulfill the meaning of Wonderful Counselor, Mighty God, Everlasting Father, and Prince of Peace. That He was not called by these names during His earthly ministry is beside the point and should not disturb us. These names are descriptions of His character. They are merely descriptive titles of who He is.

2. The Word "Name" Is Singular

When something is out of sync, we tend to notice it because it stands out as odd or unusual. That's the case in our second observation with regard to the phrase, "And His name will be called . . ." What is striking here is that the word "name" is singular, while the rest of the verse goes on to give a list of several names. We would expect this introductory phrase to say, "And His *names* [plural] will be called," with the four names—Wonderful Counselor, Mighty God, Eternal Father, and Prince of Peace—following. Instead the word "name" is singular, and that is an oddity of grammar. It stands out as unusual.

Earlier, in Isaiah 7:14, the prophet mentioned that a name (singular) would be given to this special Child: "Behold, a virgin will be with child and bear a son, and she will call his *name* Immanuel" (emphasis added). In this verse there is only one name, Immanuel, as would be expected by the fact that the word "name" is singular. We expect one name, and that's what we get. When Isaiah wrote chapter 9, verse 6, however, he violated this grammatical expectation and gave four double names to the Child after writing that "His name [singular] will be called . . ." Isaiah is an astute grammarian, and so we can assume that he is making a special point with regard to the name of this Child.

On first thought, we all know that a person's name can have multiple parts. My name is Daniel Robert Hayden. That's my name, singular, and yet my name has three parts to it. Most people can identify with this, as it is common to give three and even four or more parts to a name. This is *not*, however, what Isaiah was saying. The four couplets are not simply four parts of the Child's name. They are four separate designations with four separate orientations to who the Child will be.

An illustration of this grammatical peculiarity (a singular name with multiple designations) can be found in Matthew's account of the Great Commission at the end of his Gospel. Just before Jesus ascended into heaven He said to His disciples, "Go therefore and make disciples of all the nations, baptizing them in the *name* of the Father and the Son and the Holy Spirit . . ." (Matt. 28:19, emphasis mine). Here Jesus uses the word "name" (singular) to describe a plurality of persons: the Father, the Son, and the Holy Spirit. What he seems to be saying is that God is both one God with one name, and at the same time three Persons with three separate identities. This, along with other evidences from the Bible, is the basis for the doctrine that God is a tri-unity—or Trinity. There are three Persons in the Godhead, but there is only one God. Therefore, He has a singular name, and a plurality within that name.

This, then, appears to be what Isaiah is saying. The Child will only be one Person, but there will be numerous ways of identifying Him. Yet each of these designations will constitute only one name. As W. A. Criswell discovered, there are 256 designations in Scripture for this Child, all of which are glorious facets of His one name.

While traveling to Israel, my wife and I have often taken our tour group to one of Israel's diamond processing centers. Israel is in fact one of the largest processors of diamonds in the world. Upon entering the facility, our group would view a documentary movie on how diamonds are mined and processed for measuring and cutting. Then we would be ushered through an area where artisans were actually working on the gems by cutting the facets, as well as polishing and inspecting each diamond. We were shown how a diamond is cut for the purpose of enhancing its brilliance and maximizing its value. We learned that each facet of a diamond is measured and precisely cut to allow a different aspect of the diamond to come forth. Then later as the diamond is turned, those facets will radiate the inner beauty of an individual gem.

I would suggest to you that this is exactly the sort of phenomenon we have here with the word "name." There is one name for the Child of Isaiah's prophecy, the Person we know as Jesus Christ. And yet there are numerous facets to that name, all of which are precisely cut and polished to reveal the wonderful beauty of who He is. Actually, there are 256 facets to His name—a diversity of qualities and characteristics that magnify His wondrous perfections.

3. The Emphasis Is on the Quality of His Character

There is a third observation on this verse that affects how we understand this fourfold name of Christ. None of the four couplets in Isaiah 9:6 that follow "And His name will be called" have a definite article preceding them. The lack of the word *the* here is called *anarthrous*, which means "without the article" (as opposed to *articular*, which means "with the article"). In other words, there is no *the* before any of the four names in this verse.

The King James Version at this point fosters a bit of confusion by including the word "the" before three of the names: "The mighty God, The everlasting Father, The Prince of Peace." But the article is not there in the Hebrew original and is better reflected by the New American Standard Bible and New International Version, which say His name will be called "Wonderful Counselor, Mighty God, Eternal [Everlasting] Father, Prince of Peace."

Jehovah's Witnesses make a big issue of this *anarthrous* construction in Isaiah 9:6 because they want to diminish the effect of the term "Mighty God" as applied to Jesus Christ. They, of course, do not believe in the full deity of Christ—that He is co-equal and co-eternal with the Father. Instead, they teach that He was a created being and is therefore merely a little god. That is why they like to stress the point that Isaiah 9:6 does not say that He was "*The* Mighty God," but rather, they claim, "a mighty god," supplying the English indefinite article, *a*.

This is a common ploy on the part of the Jehovah's Witnesses to nullify the biblical teaching on the deity of Christ. For instance, in John 1:1 they make the same argument from the Greek text, where the Bible says, "the Word was God." Here again the article is not used in the original; so they again supply the English indefinite article *a* to say, "the word was a god." This is how they reflect the *anarthrous* construction in both the

Hebrew and Greek languages. Using the English language, they supply "a," saying it has an indefinite meaning. The problem with this, however, is that they are wrong—dead wrong! They are, in fact, exposing their ignorance of the Hebrew and Greek languages.

In neither the Hebrew nor the Greek is there an indefinite article. These languages simply do not have *a* or *an* as a means of expressing indefiniteness. The article and the lack of an article is used for a different purpose in these languages: When the article is used (*articular* construction), there is an emphasis on the specific *identity* of the object; but when the article is not used (*anarthrous* construction), the emphasis is on the *qualitative* meaning of the object. This important point is clarified in a manual of Greek grammar by H. E. Dana and Julius Mantey in which they discuss the *anarthrous* omission of the word *the* in Greek grammar:

> Sometimes with a noun . . . the article is not used. This places stress upon the qualitative aspect of the noun rather than its mere identity. An object of thought may be conceived of from two points of view: as to *identity* or *quality*. To convey the first point of view the Greek uses the article; for the second the anarthrous construction is used.[3]

Let me give you a homey illustration. Suppose you were having a festive dinner of turkey with all the trimmings, and as you slice the carving knife into the turkey, someone says, "He is carving the turkey." That statement highlights the identity of the particular thing being carved. It is *the* turkey. But suppose someone else said, "Hey, I think we're having turkey." That's not a reference to a particular turkey but rather to the qualitative nature of the type of meat being served: It is turkey as opposed to ham or beef. When the article is used, the emphasis is on the particular identity of the bird on the table; but when the article is not used, the emphasis is on the qualitative nature of the type of meat being served.

Well, that's exactly what we have in John 1 and in Isaiah 9. In John 1:1 we have the statement, "the Word was God." There is no definite article; but this is not a license to insert the indefinite article *a* as in English. Rather, the Greek language is putting emphasis on the *quality* of Godness. In other words, the Word has the quality of being God. You see, when we understand the Greek usage of this *anarthrous* construction, we see that the text is actually making a strong assertion that the Word is everything that is true of God. It is exactly the opposite of what the Jehovah Witnesses would like us to think.

Now the same is true in the descriptive couplets of Isaiah 9:6: Wonderful Counselor, Mighty God, Eternal Father, Prince of Peace. In the Hebrew language, as in the Greek, there is no indefinite article, and again the emphasis is on the quality of the various aspects of His name. It is not that He is *a* Mighty God, as though He were one of many. It is rather that He is everything that the Mighty God is—He possesses the quality of Mighty God. The same is true for every other designation in this verse. Not one of them has the article; so each of them is a strong emphasis on some special *quality* of His nature.

This is the grammatically correct way to understand this passage and its four couplets. The Child who was born, the Son who was given, on whose shoulder the government will rest, is also *Wonderful Counselor*—the ultimate Counselor whose counsel is a wonder to behold. He is *Mighty God*—the almighty, omnipotent Creator of the universe. He is "*Everlasting Father*" (NKJV)—the unique Savior who alone holds the key to eternal life. And He is *Prince of Peace*—the only Person who can bring true peace to this world and to every human heart. According to Isaiah, the Messiah will be all of these things; and according to the New Testament, Jesus is the fulfillment of Isaiah's prophecy.

Before leaving this subject, I would like to ask you a personal question. Do you know these qualities of our Lord, and is He special to *you* in these areas of your life? Consider, for instance, that people today are desperately looking for good counselors who can solve their personal problems. Counseling is big business in our society, and it has even become a major ministry in the Christian community. Without question, counselors have been used of God, and we need to be grateful for this blessing. But do you realize that Jesus is the *most wonderful counselor of all*, and that His counsel is freely given in His Word? In your difficulties, as you prayerfully read His Word and trust the Holy Spirit to use it in your life, you can experience His counseling wonder. It's true! Read His Word, study His Word, and meditate upon His Word. If you truly want to have the counsel that reaches into your heart and changes your life, then by all means go to Jesus and listen to His Word. Learn to know Him, and rely on Him in this way.

Jesus is also *Mighty God*, and there is nothing He cannot do in your life. Now I know that sometimes He chooses not to work supernaturally. In fact, it is a mistake to presume that the Lord will always perform miracles to get us out of jams or solve our dilemmas. But when we trust Him and obey His Word, He has promised to bless our lives (Prov. 28:20; Gal. 6:7-9). Literally, thousands of Christians can attest to Christ's special work on their behalf. Sometimes He works in the mundane, routine, day-to-day events of life to produce extraordinary results. Occasionally it is a spectacular manifestation of His power on our behalf. But always He is Mighty God who dwells in our lives by His Spirit. We can experience a special confidence, optimism, and joy when we understand this principle. So, do you know Him that way too?

What about *Eternal Father,* or more literally *Father of Eternity?* This is Jesus' role as our Savior, for He gives to us eternal life as a result of our believing in His name. Do you realize that Jesus is the bridge over troubled waters, over the chasm of sin and destruction and eternal damnation? It is Jesus who gathers us in His arms and leads us into eternal bliss with God. Jesus alone is the Father of Eternity. Do you possess this eternal hope through Him?

And then there is *Prince of Peace.* Have you discovered the peace of God in your heart through intimate fellowship with the Prince of Peace? Or are you agitated and disturbed? Do you get upset and fret about life? How much better it is to trust the One who is the absolute zenith of peace! To those who commit their lives to Him in thankful prayer, He gives a peace that "surpasses all understanding" (Philippians 4:6-7, NKJV). That's the promise He makes in His Word—*to you*!

Oh, how important it is to realize that these names truly reflect the glory of our Savior and that these qualities are available to us as we fellowship with Him.

4. "Jesus" Is the Essence of His Name

The fourth and last observation has to do with the one name that incorporates all of the others and gathers their meanings into a single essence. Essence is the "fundamental nature or most important quality (of something)."[4] The essence of a fragrance, for instance, is what remains when everything else is distilled or extracted from the compound substance. In like manner, when we distill the multiple names of our Lord down to a basic essence, there is one name that remains—and that name is Jesus.

Let me illustrate this from an earlier prophecy of Isaiah:

"Behold, a virgin will be with child and bear a son, and she will call His name Immanuel" (7:14). We have looked at this verse a number of times, but here I want to call your attention to the way the name Immanuel is used in the birth account of Christ.

When the angel told Joseph that the virgin-born Child should be named Jesus (Matt. 1:21), he seemed to contradict the intention of Isaiah's prophecy. Isaiah said the Child's name would be Immanuel; but the angel said his name was to be Jesus. Which name is it—Immanuel or Jesus? The answer is found in the explanation given by the angel when the Child was named Jesus. Matthew tells us this actually fulfilled the prophecy of Isaiah that His name would be Immanuel (Matt. 1:22-23). Let's delve further into what the angel meant.

The name Jesus actually means "one who saves," which is why the angel gave this explanation: "for it is He who will save His people from their sins" (Matt. 1:21). Now in order for that to happen, two things had to be true of this Child. First, He had to be sinless in order to be a qualified substitute for others; and second, He had to be infinite in order to represent more than one person as a substitute. Of course, there is only one being in the universe who is both sinless and infinite, and that is God. Therefore, in order to be *Jesus* (meaning "Savior"), the Child had to be *God among us*. That is exactly what *Immanuel* means. So that is why Gabriel could say that naming the Child Jesus would be the fulfillment of the prophecy of Isaiah that the Child would be called Immanuel.

Let me back up for a moment and explain more fully these two divine requirements for the Savior. First of all, as I have already mentioned (this is really important), the Savior had to be sinless. That is why Christ's arrival on earth had to be by means of a virgin birth. If Joseph had been the natural father, Jesus would have inherited the sin of Adam in the same way that all humans do (Rom. 5:12). And if Jesus inherited the sin of Adam, then He would have been under the curse that has been upon the whole human race. Consequently He would have had to die for His own sin, precluding Him from dying for the sins of others. He had to be born sinless; and that is why, as the Son of God, the Savior had to be born of a virgin. As God, the Savior is sinless; and as a virgin-born Child, He remained sinless.

In the second place, the Savior had to be infinite in order for His sacrifice to have an infinite value. Just think of it! From Adam to the last person who will ever live on this earth, there are billions of people—and every one of them needs a Savior. Furthermore, these billions of people have all committed sins—in all, an enormous number of iniquities. How many sins have you committed? Well, if you are like me, you've quit counting. Then there is the fact that the Bible tells us that the wages of sin is eternal death (Rom. 6:23); so the punishment for each of those billions of people is an eternal punishment. Eternity, you understand, is infinity with respect to time.

So there you have it. An infinite number of people who have committed an infinite number of sins, to be paid for over an infinite amount of time. Therefore, no one could be the Savior of mankind without an infinite capacity to deal with the problem.

Years ago my five-year-old grandson, Nolan, and I were riding in the car together when suddenly he turned to me and said, "Grandpa, you know what I want?" Somewhat intrigued I answered, "What?" "Infinite money!" he replied happily. "Hey, you've got to be kidding. Where'd you learn that word *infinite*?" I asked him. "Well, I don't know, but *infinite* means it doesn't stop. Isn't that right, Grandpa?"

You bet. That's exactly what it means, and he was exactly right. Infinity means it never ends; and that's true of every aspect of God. He is omnipotent—there is no end to His strength. He is omniscient—there's no limit to His knowledge. He's omnipresent—there is no place He is not. He's omni-everything! It is a quality of His nature that He is infinite. Therefore as God, Jesus could pay for an infinite number of sins, committed by an infinite number of people, for an infinite amount of time. And that is why the Savior had to be Immanuel, "God with us." And that is key to the explanation of the angel that the name *Jesus* would fulfill the prophecy that His name would be *Immanuel*.

Now what is true for Isaiah 7:14 and the name Immanuel is also true for Isaiah 9:6 and the four couplets that comprise His name. For you see, if He is Jesus, the Savior, then He is absolutely the Counseling Wonder. If He is Jesus, then He is also Mighty God. If He is Jesus, then He is the Father of Eternity and the Prince of Peace. Jesus is indeed the essence of His name.

FINAL THOUGHTS

Today the world is looking for a savior—someone to solve the personal, corporate, and international problems of the world. The virgin-born Child of Isaiah's prophecy is the only solution because that Child is Immanuel, "God with us." In the course of time it was revealed that this Child was the virgin-born son of Mary, Jesus, the Savior of the world. He is known by many designations in the Scriptures, but the essence of who He is is *Jesus*. He is God, having come to earth to save us.

As we conclude this chapter, I want to encourage you, if you do not know Jesus Christ as your personal Savior, to reflect upon His name—*Jesus*—the only Person in the universe who can save you from your sin. Have you personally confessed your sin to God and placed your trust in Christ? If not, I would encourage you to pray this little prayer: "O God, I know that I am a sinner. I thank You that Jesus Christ died for my sin. Lord Jesus, come into my heart and save me." On the authority of God's Word, He will do just that.

For those who know Jesus Christ as Savior, perhaps you won't mind if I challenge you to learn more of the facets of our Savior's glory. Set aside time to consider the richness of His character as it is reflected in these four marvelous designations of His name. As you meditate on these truths of His Word, ask the Spirit of God to fill your heart with wonder and adoration for Jesus. Let the meaning of His name filter into your life and captivate your soul. Then thank Him for all that He is to you. As you do these things, you will learn more fully the meaning of true joy and inner peace.

4

UNRAVELING THE MESS

Finally, Someone with Answers

". . . Wonderful Counselor . . ."
ISAIAH 9:6

Charles slouched in the comfortable office chair and breathed a heavy sigh, revealing the burden that lay on his heart. Things had not gone well over the last several months, which was an understatement of what he was feeling. Wrong decisions had led to crippling entanglements that were threatening to destroy all that he valued in life. The ever-present question floated through his mind: *How could it all have come to this?* But he knew the answer. It wasn't difficult to figure out. What had started as a simple escapade of self-indulgence had suddenly become an unmanageable storm of unexpected complications. He was angry at himself and extremely embarrassed to expose the truth of what he had done. Yet he needed help, which is why he had come to the pastor for counseling. Charles took a deep breath and began to speak as the pastor settled in for what he knew would be a long and difficult session.

That is a real-life situation, and I was that counselor. As a pastor I often sat in heavy, emotionally-laden sessions listening to confused and heartbroken people. Counseling is big business in our society, and that is equally true for the church. It seems that our humanistic, secular, existential culture is a deteriorating culture; and people are less able to cope with the problems of life than ever before. Self-indulgence and personal fulfillment have replaced a sacrificial spirit and self-discipline. People are encouraged to be more lustful than loving, and more greedy than gracious. Superficial fun is everybody's aspiration, as illustrated by the bumper sticker, "A bad day of fishing is better than a good day at the office." It's a crazy world out there—and it's getting more insane every day! No wonder counseling has skyrocketed to a place of prominence as a career choice.

When I was teaching at a Bible college, it was interesting for me to observe the rise of counseling as an academic pursuit. A number of years ago only a few courses were offered in the basics of Christian counseling. Today students can major in counseling and pursue graduate degrees in counseling at that college. What was particularly disappointing to me, however, was the realization that counseling as a major had surpassed a career choice in missions. The college is still known for its preparation of missionaries, but it is now better known for its training of counselors. That is certainly a reflection upon our times. It is a classic case of supply and demand.

The questions that are asked in all of this are: What is the best counsel? Where can I go to get it? That is the issue of our times, and that is the subject of this chapter. The bottom-line answer to those questions is simply this: The Word of God is the best counsel, and Jesus Christ is the foremost counselor. After all, Isaiah tells us He is the "Wonderful Counselor."

More than New Year's resolutions, we need a renovation of life. As much as any other time in the history of the world, we are in need of wise counsel. Not the humanistic counsel of secular psychology, but the divine counsel of the Word of God. The fact that Jesus is the Counseling Wonder means that the role of the biblical counselor is primarily to help the counselee understand Christ's counsel.

JESUS CHRIST IS A WONDERFUL COUNSELOR

"And His name will be called Wonderful Counselor . . ."

As we begin, we unfortunately have to work through a translation difficulty. The question that arises is this: Is *Wonderful Counselor* two separate qualities (wonderful and counselor), or is this one grand description (Wonderful Counselor)? Isaiah uses two words here, and in some translations these words are separated so as to indicate two names, whereas in other translations the two words are put together to form just one name. So the question before us is, "Which is it— one name or two?"

The major tradition for seeing two names centers around the King James Version of the Bible. In the KJV there is a comma separating the two words, so that each represents a different name for the Child of Isaiah's prophecy. In other words, His name is Wonderful, and His name is Counselor. Apparently this is due to the fact that the King James translators followed the tradition of the Latin Vulgate (the official Bible of the Catholic Church in the Middle Ages), which also divides the two words.

If you consult commentaries on this question, you discover that a few scholars do prefer to keep the two names separate. For instance, W. E. Vine's opinion in his commentary on Isaiah is that "these two are not to be combined into one phrase as if the first was an adjective describing the Counselor as wonderful: each is a noun."[1] Well, in a moment I want to show you that's not exactly true; each is *not* a noun, but that's his comment.

Another example comes from Franz Delitzsch, a very popular Hebrew commentator. In his commentary on these two words in Isaiah 9:6 he says, "The first name . . . is not to be taken in connection with the next word." Then he admits, "though this construction might seem to commend itself."[2] He then proceeds to give four reasons why they *should* go together, after which he merely concludes, "whereas there is nothing at all to prevent our taking [them] as two separate names."[3] Well to me, his vacillation on this issue is a little confusing.

On the other side of the debate, more recent translations (such as the New American Standard and the New International Version) put the two words together as a compound name, Wonderful Counselor. Actually I think they have good reasons for doing so.

Let me give six observations that support the conclusion that the best translation of Isaiah 9:6 is to regard Wonderful Counselor as a single compound name.

1. Counselor is a participle. I hope you will forgive me for another reference to grammar, but it really is a great help in understanding this phrase. Remember W. E. Vine's comment that the two words were nouns? Well, the truth of the matter is that *wonderful* (or literally, wonder) is a noun, but *counselor* is a participle. A participle is a verbal adjective and in this case is more accurately translated "counseling." In English we generally put *-ing* on the end of a word to indicate that it is a participle (i.e., running, eating, etc.). Now it's true that participles can sometimes be used in a substantive sense (like nouns), but even then they will retain the verbal adjective idea (e.g., swimming takes a lot of energy). So Isaiah literally said that the Child would be called *Counseling Wonder*. His activity of counseling would be a wonder to behold.

2. *The Masoretic Text accentuates it this way.* The Masoretic Text is the traditional Hebrew Scriptures of the Old Testament. It is called the Masoretic Text because it was compiled from existing Hebrew manuscripts by the Masoretes, a group of Hebrew scholars during the period of A.D. 600-1000. One of their significant contributions was to develop a system of vowel signs and accents that they added to the Hebrew text to preserve the proper pronunciation of words. The reason for this is that the Hebrew language is basically consonantal. In other words, if you picked up a Hebrew newspaper from Israel today, the words would be only consonants—no vowels. Furthermore, the Masoretes developed accent marks to indicate how words went together and to demonstrate the flow of thought. Well, this official text of the Hebrew Scriptures put the words *wonder* and *counselor* together as a couplet in the same fashion as Mighty God, Everlasting Father, and Prince of Peace. *Wonderful Counselor* is one grand description in the Hebrew Bible, and this supports the view that the correct way to translate Isaiah 9:6 is with four compound names.

3. *The Septuagint translation puts the words together.* A third line of evidence has to do with the Septuagint, a Greek translation of the Old Testament from around 200 B.C. that was used by the apostles of Christ. In fact, the apostles quoted from the Septuagint more than they quoted from the Hebrew Scriptures. To a large extent, this was the Bible of the early New Testament church. Well, this Greek translation of the Hebrew Bible combines the words *wonder* and *counselor* into one descriptive name as well, just as the Hebrew Text of the Masoretes did.

As a little aside, there is a variation in the Septuagint text that is quite interesting. Three Greek words are used in the Septuagint to translate the two Hebrew words *Wonderful Counselor*. They are the words *great, counsel,* and *messenger.* So it literally reads, "messenger of great counsel." The word for *great* here is the Greek word *mega* (as in megabucks or megaphone). So the idea in the Septuagint, then, is that our Lord is a mega-counselor, and that is an incredible wonder!

4. *There is a remarkable symmetry* in the four couplets we are considering: Wonderful Counselor, Mighty God, Everlasting Father, Prince of Peace. Bible teachers often refer to Isaiah as "the prince of the prophets," and given his profound literary skills it is an appropriate description. Isaiah's writing has all the earmarks of a highly educated man who was very skilled in language. His Hebrew is flawless, and his poetic ability is outstanding. There is great harmony and design in all that he does. Therefore, we would expect harmony and literary balance in the four names he ascribes to the Messianic Child. To regard Wonderful Counselor as a couplet designation, then, maintains a balanced parallel with the other three couplets and establishes a wonderfully harmonious cadence. This is no little argument for putting the words *wonderful* and *counselor* together as one designation.

5. *Isaiah places these words together in a later text.* He puts these two words, *wonderful* and *counselor,* together in Isaiah 28:29. The context is agricultural as Isaiah describes God's wisdom as it relates to farming. "This also comes from the LORD of hosts," he writes, "*who* has made *His counsel wonderful* and *His* wisdom great" (emphasis added). The placement of "wonderful" and "counsel" together as one thought in this verse certainly argues for the possibility that he did the same in 9:6. Indeed, Isaiah demonstrates that he is struck by the fact that God's counsel is truly wonderful.

6. *Many commentators see the name as a couplet.* I have mentioned that a few scholars such as W. E. Vine and Franz Delitzsch do see the two words as separate names. Yet other significant voices argue that Wonderful Counselor is in fact one compound name. Edward J. Young, for instance, has written one of the most outstanding commentaries on the book of Isaiah. In this three-volume set he makes a strong case for the words going together as a single designation.[4] Another celebrated Hebrew scholar, Merrill F. Unger, who produced the popular *Unger's Bible Dictionary* and *Unger's Bible Handbook*, also sees the words as one name, stating that it is literally "a wonder of a counselor."[5] John Martin agrees that the words are a compound concept. In *The Bible Knowledge Commentary*, produced by Dallas Seminary, he declares, "He will have four descriptive names that will reveal His character"[6] (as opposed to five, when the words wonderful and counselor are taken separately). So we see that there are excellent scholarly sources for understanding *Wonderful Counselor* as a single name.

Summary

Well, there you have it—six reasons to take the couplet *Wonderful Counselor* as one compound name. A quick review reminds us that the word translated "Counselor" is actually a participle that suggests the type of wonder that He is—He is a Counseling Wonder. The official Hebrew Scriptures, as represented by the Masoretic Text, regard the words as a unit, as does the Septuagint. Then in addition to the grammatical and textual considerations, when Wonderful Counselor is seen as a couplet we find a remarkable symmetry with the other three compound names of Mighty God, Everlasting Father, and Prince of Peace. It is what we expect from a skilled writer such as Isaiah. Furthermore, Isaiah himself combines the words "wonderful" and "counsel" in a later passage (28:29), demonstrating that God's counsel is indeed a wonder. In the light of these things then, it is no wonder that significant Bible scholars understand these words as a compound name.

So having dealt with the translation issue, we are now ready to consider the meaning of this incredible name of our Lord. He is surely a Counseling Wonder, and we want to probe some of the spiritual ramifications of this magnificent truth as it relates to our desperate need for counsel.

JESUS CHRIST IS A COUNSELING WONDER

Now that this preliminary study is behind us, let's consider the meaning and implications of the fact that the Child of Isaiah's prophecy was to be known as *Wonderful Counselor*. What does it mean that Jesus Christ is a Counseling Wonder, and what are the implications of that truth for His people—for you and me? As a preliminary thought, consider these words of David Garland:

> He is to be called "a Wonder of a Counselor." He is to bear this name because the counsel which He gives will be above the counsel of ordinary men. It will be the counsel of Yahweh [Jehovah], and therefore wonderful.[7]

So let's look at each part of this compound name *Wonderful Counselor*. First of all, let's consider what it means that His counsel is called *wonderful*.

Our Lord Is a Wonder to Behold

The first word of this couplet name in Isaiah 9:6 is the word "wonderful." Because it is the first word in the Hebrew text, it indicates an emphasis on the wonder of who He is and what He will do. The Hebrew word is the word *pele*, a noun that means "wonder" in the sense of "wonderful thing" or "miracle."

Now when you think of the word *wonderful* in English, what does that bring to your mind? Usually the word *wonderful* carries the idea of something especially nice—something beautiful or pleasant with which you are particularly pleased. But the Hebrew word *pele* is more intense than that. *Pele* has the idea of being full of wonder. It's more than a pleasant experience. Rather, it's like a thunder and lightning storm! It's a wonder to behold, leaving the beholder full of wonder. It's wonder-*full*.

Those who are sports enthusiasts may remember the brilliant Brazilian soccer star Pele (pronounced *pe-lé*). Some consider him to have been the best soccer player in the world ever. His feats of athleticism and incredible agility were absolute wonders as he entertained soccer fans game after game. Of course, it is just a coincidence that his name is spelled the same as the Hebrew word *pele*, but he is a good illustration of the meaning of the word. "Wonderful" in this verse is something spectacular, not just something nice.

When Moses and the children of Israel came to the Red Sea with the Egyptians behind them and the Sea before them, Moses stretched out his staff over the Sea and called upon the name of Jehovah. Then an amazing thing happened: The waters parted, and the children of Israel walked through on dry land. That was a *pele*. It was a wonder!

When Joshua fought the enemies of Israel in the Valley of Aijalon, he needed more time to complete the victory because the sun was going down. So God caused the sun to stand still in support of Joshua's conquest. Somehow God caused the rotation of the entire earth to slow down in support of one military endeavor, demonstrating His sovereign power over the universe. That, my friend, was a *pele*. It was a wonder!

Elijah stood on Mount Carmel in the midst of the prophets of Baal, who were frustrated in their attempts to induce their god to light the fire of sacrifice. Then Elijah called upon the living God, and fire poured out of heaven, consuming the water and the sacrifice. It was an awesome scene. It was a *pele*—a wonder!

Are you beginning to get the point? To be filled with wonder is to be struck by awe. That's the idea of this Hebrew word, *pele*.

There is a great illustration of this in Judges 13:1-18, which recounts an experience that Manoah and his wife had. They were the parents of Samson, and on this occasion they were confronted by the angel of the Lord (many Bible teachers believe that the angel of the Lord was an appearance of Christ before He became a man, as recorded in the Gospels). At any rate, the appearance of this heavenly being was amazing: "his appearance was like the appearance of the angel of God, very awesome . . ." (v. 6). Well, in the story Manoah asks the angel a question: "What is your name, so that when your words come *to pass*, we may honor you?" (v. 17). The angel of the Lord replied, "Why do you ask my name, seeing it is wonderful [*pele*]?" (v. 18). There it is! "Wonderful" is a descriptive name for the One from heaven, and even as a single name it has great meaning. It means that He is absolutely awesome!

The Child who was born and the Son who was given, according to Isaiah, would be *pele*—He would be a wonder. And this was certainly true of Jesus. His virgin birth was a *wonder*, His sinless life was a *wonder*, and His teaching and miracles were *wonders*. His victorious life was a *wonder*, as were His sacrificial death and glorious resurrection. When Jesus turned the water to wine, it was a *wonder*. When He fed five thousand people with a little boy's lunch, that was a *wonder*. When He healed the paralytic, and when He made the blind to see, those were *wonders* too. When

He spoke into the grave of Lazarus and called him forth after four days of death, it was an incredible *wonder*!

We certainly have to admit, then, that this single designation is indeed fitting as a descriptive word for everything about the Lord. Those who see this as a single name really do have a point: His name is *wonder*—full of wonder—Wonderful!

Take a moment to consider your own response to this aspect of our Lord's name. Can you look into the manger of Bethlehem and not be filled with awe? Can you visualize God as a baby and not be absolutely blown away? Can you contemplate the meaning of the name *Jesus*—that He came for the express purpose of dying for your sins—and not be flabbergasted to the core of your being? Wow! All of this is absolutely amazing. It is the most incredible thing that has ever happened on earth, and His love for you is at the heart of it all.

These are the kinds of reflections that should produce within us a spirit of worship. As you ponder these thoughts with me from Isaiah's prophecy, perhaps each of us should prostrate our soul before Him and offer to Him the sacrifice of our praise (Heb. 13:15). He is truly wonderful and worthy of all honor.

Our Lord Is a Counselor to Be Sought

In addition to being a wonder, our Lord is also a counselor; and according to Isaiah 9:6 these words are to be thought of as a single unit. Although Jesus Christ is a wonder in many things, Isaiah is telling us specifically that He is a *wonder in counsel*.

This second word, "Counselor," as we noted earlier in this chapter, is a Hebrew participle. This means that it has the properties of both a verb (action) and an adjective (modifier). It comes from the verb *ya ats*, which means "to advise, to counsel, to admonish," and it plays the role of an adjective modifying the noun "wonder." So we are being told what kind of a wonder Jesus is—He's a counseling wonder. This is how we are to understand this word.

Think with me for a moment about another passage, Isaiah 11:1-5, which speaks of the righteous reign of the Person who would have the government on His shoulder. The subject is the same, and the Person is the same. It is the Child who would be born, the Son who would be given, who is here called the stem of Jesse, the branch from his roots. Jesse was the father of King David and therefore ultimately the one from whom the Messiah would come. Here is what Isaiah said about this Person:

> 1 Then a shoot will spring from the stem of Jesse,
>   And a branch from his roots will bear fruit.
> 2 And the Spirit of the LORD will rest on Him,
>   The spirit of wisdom and understanding,
>   The spirit of counsel and strength,
>   The spirit of knowledge and fear of the LORD.
> 3 And He will delight in the fear of the LORD,
>   And He will not judge by what His eyes see,
>   Nor make a decision by what His ears hear;
> 4 But with righteousness He will judge the poor,
>   And decide with fairness for the afflicted of the earth;
>   And He will strike the earth with the rod of His mouth,
>   And with the breath of His lips He will slay the wicked.
> 5 Also righteousness will be the belt about His loins,
>   And faithfulness the belt about His waist.

What a glorious Person we see here—One who is full of righteousness, full of faithfulness, who will do what is right, and who will be trustworthy. Isaiah also says that a sevenfold spirit will be upon Him. In Proverbs 9:1 we read, "Wisdom has built her house, she has hewn out her seven pillars." Well, here in Isaiah we find the seven pillars of wisdom reflected in these seven characteristics of the Spirit's work. This ruler from the stem of Jesse will know the Spirit of the Lord, the spirit of wisdom, the spirit of understanding, the spirit of counsel, the spirit of strength, the spirit of knowledge, and the spirit of the fear of the Lord. That is what will make Him great.

Notice that right in the middle of this sevenfold spirit is "the spirit of counsel" (v. 2). This is the same word found in Isaiah 9:6—*ya ats*. It's as though His counsel is surrounded by wisdom and understanding on one side and strength and knowledge on the other side. Then encompassing them all is the Spirit of the Lord and the spirit of the fear of the Lord. Here is a Person whose counsel is indeed spectacular! It is wise counsel with great understanding. It is strong counsel that is full of knowledge. And most of all, it is the counsel of God Himself, emanating out of who He is. Here is a Counselor unlike any other the world has ever known!

One of our greatest contemporary needs is someone to counsel us with regard to our problems. I have a friend who is a physician, and one day a man in his office said to him, "We need to find someone who has the wisdom to take us into the third millennium." In reply my doctor friend simply said, "Guess what, we've found Him. His name is Jesus." Now that's the point! Jesus Christ is the Counseling Wonder. The spirit of counsel is upon Him.

Paul put it this way when speaking of Jesus in Colossians 2:3: "in whom are hidden all the treasures of wisdom and knowledge." Then again in 1 Corinthians 1:30 Paul says, "But of Him," referring to God, "you are in Christ Jesus, who became for us wisdom from God" (NKJV). You see for Paul, Christ is the essence of wisdom; and that wisdom is available to us who believe in Him. In the same vein, I love the way Paul concludes the eleventh chapter of Romans:

Oh, the depth of the riches both of the wisdom and knowledge of God! How unsearchable are His judgments and unfathomable His ways! FOR WHO HAS KNOWN THE MIND OF THE LORD, OR WHO BECAME HIS COUNSELOR? OR WHO HAS FIRST GIVEN TO HIM THAT IT MIGHT BE PAID BACK TO HIM AGAIN? For from Him and through Him and to Him are all things. To Him be the glory forever. Amen.

—vv. 33-36

Really, there is no counselor like Jesus—whether we think of counsel on an individual level or in regard to global affairs. He is the only One with sufficient answers to our problems. And one day, when the government will rest upon His shoulder, He will bring His wisdom to bear upon the needs of Planet Earth. In the meantime His wisdom is available for all who seek it.

But herein lies a concern. For much of the contemporary church today it seems that when it comes to the need for counsel, people see Jesus as their last chance instead of their first choice. To many it seems to be easier to have someone tell them what to do than to prayerfully search the Scriptures for the wisdom of Christ.

One of the reasons for this is that our existential culture has conditioned all of us to be more experience-oriented and less study-oriented. In his excellent analysis of our secular culture, Neil Postman made the observation that we have gone from a print-based culture to an image-based culture.[8] What this means essentially is that we are reading less and watching TV more. The title of his book is *Amusing Ourselves to Death*, and that's exactly what he demonstrates is happening. This phenomenon is killing our culture. And I can assure you, it is damaging the church as well.

Part of the fallout of this condition is that we are less studied and therefore less knowledgeable. In a spiritual sense we have a casual acquaintance with Jesus rather than a true and intimate acquaintance with Him. He is a convenient friend when we're in trouble, and we count on Him to bail us out at the end, but He has very little influence on the way we live our lives. He is a great counselor, but we don't know enough of His counsel for it to make a difference. That's not true of all Christians, of course; yet the observable impact of this trend upon the church has been profound.

What, then, is the answer to this dilemma? The answer is simply to buck the trend and become more serious about pursuing Christ. But you may ask, "How do I do that?" Well, there are two basic things to understand. Let me see if I can explain them to you.

1. He counsels through the work of the Holy Spirit. If Jesus Christ is the Counseling Wonder, how does He do that? When He lived on earth and interacted with people early in the first century, He counseled them because He was there. We can understand that. But He's not here now. So how can He counsel *us*? How can we know His personal counsel in a practical way? Well, the first thing we need to know is that He does it through the work of His Holy Spirit, who *is* with us.

Here we need to understand what Jesus meant when He said, "I will ask the Father, and He will give you another Helper" (John 14:16). As I mentioned in the last chapter, the word *helper* in this verse is the Greek word *parakletos*—"one called alongside" for the purpose of helping. This is also the word used for an "advocate" or lawyer who is called upon to help by means of legal counsel (cf. 1 John 2:1). In other words, this is someone who is a counselor, a helper, or an advocate.

In John 14 Jesus told His disciples that He was about to leave them, but that He would send someone else to continue the work that He had been doing. This Person, He said, would be the Holy Spirit: "But the Helper, the Holy Spirit, whom the Father will send in My name, He will teach you all things, and bring to your remembrance all that I said to you" (John 14:26). So Jesus assured His disciples that after He left, He would continue to counsel them, but He would do it by means of the Holy Spirit.

Now Jesus Christ is the Counseling Wonder. Isaiah has told us that. In the three and a half years of Jesus' earthly ministry (as recorded in the Gospels), we see Him counseling people as He gave them instruction and guidance. He was fulfilling His role as a *parakletos*, coming alongside to help. Then, as we saw in John 14:16, the disciples learned that the Holy Spirit would be given to them as "another Helper [Counselor]" to take Christ's place after He left. The word translated *another* is from the Greek word *allos*, which carries the idea of "another of the same kind." So the Holy Spirit is another *parakletos*—another Counselor of the same kind as Jesus.

In addition, notice what Jesus went on to say: "*that is* the Spirit of truth, whom the world cannot receive, because it does not behold Him or know Him, *but* you know Him because He abides with you, and will be in you" (John 14:17). Here Jesus was speaking to His disciples to prepare them for the change that was coming with Pentecost and the beginning of the Church Age. Jesus Himself would not be physically present, but the *Helper* ("Comforter," KJV) whom the Father would send "will be in you." That "you" applied to the disciples of the early church, but it also includes those of us who live today. Dwelling within anyone who truly believes in Jesus Christ is this same Holy Spirit who empowered the disciples at Pentecost (1 Cor. 6:19).

Imagine, if you will, that you have a therapist whom you have become very dependent upon for counsel. Your therapist one day tells you that he is moving away and will no longer be available to counsel you directly, but he's going to provide another therapist whose competence as a counselor is equal to his. He tells you that they grew up together, were best friends, and graduated from the same schools; so they think alike and are nearly identical in every way. Furthermore, your therapist assures you that he will share your file with the new counselor so that he will be fully aware of your history and counseling needs. Also, to your delight, your therapist mentions that he and his friend stay in close contact with one another, so that if there is any question about your situation, he will always be available as a consultant. It will be as though your therapist is still there counseling you through the new counselor. So how would you now feel? Are you worried or confident?

This scenario is similar to what Jesus did when He sent the Holy Spirit as a replacement for His ministry. The big difference, however, is that the close affinity between Jesus and the Holy Spirit is much more intimate and complete than the relationship between the therapist and his friend. The Holy Spirit is in fact identical to Jesus Christ in every way except for the fact that He is a separate Person (similar to identical twins, only more so). Actually, this identity is so complete that when the Holy Spirit indwells our lives (1 Cor. 6:19), it can be said with equal confidence that Jesus Christ Himself indwells our lives (Col. 1:27). Furthermore, Jesus also said that the whole purpose of the Holy Spirit's ministry would be to adequately and fully represent Him (John 16:13-15).

Here's the point. Even though Jesus is gone and does not have a physical presence with us today, the Holy Spirit is here now, and His presence is the same as having Jesus here. The counseling ministry of Jesus continues to be relevant to His people in each generation because the Holy Spirit represents Him in the here and now. The fact that Jesus Christ is a counseling wonder is fulfilled in the Holy Spirit's ministry to us.

2. He counsels through His Word. Every counselor counsels through his or her words. That can happen in a variety of ways—through an actual verbal encounter in a counseling session or phone call, through words in a book written by the counselor, or through words spoken on an audio/video/CD product. In every case, it is the words of the counselor that frame the content of the counsel.

It is no different with the counsel of the Counseling Wonder. Jesus is actually called *the Word* in John 1 (vv. 1-2, 14), and everything we need to know about life has been communicated by Him through His Word (2 Pet. 1:1-4), which was produced by the Holy Spirit (2 Pet. 1:21). Now it really doesn't matter if His word was spoken verbally (as when He spoke to His disciples) or in the Book He has written (as when He counsels through the Bible). The point is, He counsels through His words; and the only place you can find His words today is in the Holy Scriptures.

That is why, when the apostle Paul discusses the communicating work of the Holy Spirit, he says that the Spirit teaches by "combining spiritual *thoughts* with spiritual *words*" (1 Cor. 2:13). So you see it's through words that He communicates. Paul goes on to conclude that the product of this spiritual communication is "the mind of Christ" (1 Cor. 2:16). If someone wants to know what Christ thinks on any subject, Paul is saying, Christ's thoughts must be gleaned from His Word—the Book inspired by the Holy Spirit (2 Pet. 1:21). In other words, the counseling manual of the Counseling Wonder is the Word of God.

So let's get practical here and make some basic observations about how this process works. The Bible is a big book with a lot of sections (Pentateuch, Major Prophets, Gospels, Epistles, etc.), and an incredible number of stories. So the question arises, "How do I go about finding His counsel with regard to my particular situation?"

Let's begin by getting a grasp on the general framework of His wonderful counsel. When Jesus said that He would send His Holy Spirit to be *another Helper* or Counselor, He said that the Spirit would endeavor to communicate three things. In John 16:8 He said, "And He, when He comes, will convict the world concerning sin, and righteousness, and judgment." Now I want to suggest to you that this is the essence of counseling.

(1) *Concerning sin*: That's the word Christ uses for what is wrong. This is the first thing a counselor endeavors to show his counselees—what they've done wrong, where they went astray, what they're doing to hurt themselves.

(2) *And righteousness*: This is the biblical word for what is right. The next thing of importance in counseling is to figure out how to get back on track—how to fix what's wrong by discovering what is right.

(3) *And judgment*: This simply refers to the fact that there are consequences to our choices. All counseling situations involve choices between what is good and what is bad, what is right and what is wrong. Therefore, if we choose sin, there will be the consequences of judgment (life in a deteriorating spiral); but if we choose righteousness, we will reap blessing and well-being. There is a definite consequence to every moral choice.

So there we have it. This is the counseling work of the Holy Spirit, whom Christ sent to counsel on His behalf. Therefore in a general sense, when we study the Word of God, we discover the perspective of Christ on things that are wrong, things that are right, and the consequences of choosing between what is right and what is wrong.

The Bible as a whole book reflects the importance of moral choices. "For he who sows to his flesh," the Bible says, "will of the flesh reap corruption, but he who sows to the Spirit will of the Spirit reap everlasting life" (Galatians 6:8, NKJV). That is the basis of counseling—helping people understand that sowing and reaping has affected their lives. And nobody does this better than the Holy Spirit speaking on behalf of Christ in the Word of God.

Now the Bible doesn't just speak about the good and bad of life in a general way. Every conceivable situation that we as human beings encounter in our crazy, mixed-up world is addressed in one way or another by the Scriptures. Whether it's finances or interpersonal relationships or marriage issues or family dynamics or personal quirks, the Bible has a lot of specific things to say. That, in fact, is what the stories of the Bible are all about—they are real illustrations of real situations in the lives of real people. Our responsibility is to systematically study these specific things so that we are knowledgeable concerning the wonderful counsel of the Lord.

You see, you can't just read the Bible haphazardly or go to church and hear it occasionally and then expect to connect with Christ's joyful counsel. It requires a degree of concentration and attentiveness that is quite beyond merely reading the Bible through in a year. As a counselee must pay attention to what the counselor is saying, so the person who goes to the Word of God for Christ's wonderful counsel must concentrate on what the Spirit of God is saying. A casual approach to Bible reading will never cut it. Serious Bible study on a specific subject of concern, with prayerful dependence on the working of the Holy Spirit to implement the counsel of Christ's Word in a life situation, is what will produce results.

Here is where each of us needs to make a decision. Are you spending time in the Word of God in a specific and consistent way? Do you know what God says about the matter of finances, for instance—a big subject in today's society? Do you know that Christ taught more parables on the subject of money than on any other single subject? The rest of the Bible (for example, the book of Proverbs) is full of Christ's counsel on that subject as well. So do you know what His counsel is concerning the way to handle your finances? If not, it's not because He hasn't said it—it's because you haven't read it (at least with careful attentiveness).

Now what is true concerning Christ's counsel on money is also true about His counsel on every other topic. It's all there if you're interested enough to sit and listen to the voice of the Holy Spirit through the Word of God.

A FINAL WORD TO COUNSELORS

A number of years ago I became concerned about the growing frequency of marital problems in our church. A few marriages had already ended in separation or divorce, while scores of other couples were struggling in their relationships. So I invited a well-known Christian counselor from a major Christian college to conduct a marriage and family enrichment seminar for our people. We met on a Friday night and all day Saturday—six sessions in all—and I was encouraged to see that it was well attended.

My encouragement soon turned to concern, however, as I began to monitor what the counselor was saying. He was engaging and fun to listen to, with a lot of common sense and cute things to remember. What struck me, though, was what he was *not* saying. Never once in the six hours of instruction did he open the Bible. Oh, occasionally he would throw in a verse to prove his point, but there was no sense of "thus saith the Lord." There was more psychology than Bible, and more quotes from the "experts" than from the Word of God. It wasn't that his counsel was bad or wrong; it just never got around to being wonderful counsel. Why? Because he never saw himself as being primarily a mouthpiece for the Wonderful Counselor.

A debate has been raging within the Christian community over the last several decades concerning the place of psychology in Christian counseling. Many so-called Christian counselors have simply added biblical terminology to the secular concepts of psychology, and the end result is that they have psychologized the faith. Others merely throw Bible verses at a problem in a simplistic approach to complicated issues. But in my opinion, very few have probed Isaiah's assertion that Jesus Christ is a Counseling Wonder. What Isaiah seems to be saying is not that Jesus offers good counsel that should be taken seriously, but that Jesus' counsel is so outstanding and so excellent that it totally eclipses all other forms of counseling! In light of that, I would suggest that every Christian counselor should be first and foremost a careful Bible expositor.

Let me share a personal note here. I have a college degree in psychology and a seminary degree in theology and over thirty years of pastoral counseling experience. In addition, I taught college-level pastoral counseling for four years in a Bible college. And if there is one thing I have learned in all of this, it is that Christ through His Word is completely sufficient for every life situation. It's purely a matter of understanding the Word correctly and applying it wisely.

Please understand what I am saying. It is not that the tools of psychology are totally irrelevant or inapplicable, for there is wisdom to be found in the ability to diagnose and analyze on the psychological level. Nor is it to minimize the truly complicated issues of deep emotional impairment, physiological imbalances, and psychotic disorders that may require professional and medical help. But I am suggesting that there can be no ultimate wisdom in secular psychology's remedial solutions because these solutions do not include a consideration of the spiritual dimension of life. The world's wisdom is like fighting a cold with a handkerchief. It may mop up some of the symptoms, but it doesn't begin to deal with the root cause of the problem. In the deepest sense, psychology doesn't see the fundamental problem of the human dilemma (sin and man's alienation from God), and therefore it cannot begin to comprehend the only adequate solution (salvation in Christ and the therapeutic application of His Word). That's not overly simplistic. It is the essence of wisdom.

This is not the place for a full disclosure of the shortcomings of contemporary Christian counseling. I just want to raise a voice of encouragement to all Christian counselors that the counsel of Jesus is not only superior—it is truly spectacular and awesome. By all means, become an avid student of the Bible, and learn to understand the working of the Spirit of God; then you will discover a realm of counseling that is more wonderful than anything you have ever known!

Jesus *is* the Counseling Wonder. He counsels with His wonderful words of life as found in the incredible Word of God, and He changes lives by the powerful working of His Holy Spirit who specializes in the work of regeneration. Our job as counselors is simply to represent Him well by being faithful to His Word and by leading every counselee into an intimate relationship with Christ.

5

"You Ain't Seen Nothin' Yet!"

An Amazing Person with the Powers of God

". . . Mighty God . . ."

ISAIAH 9:6

Do you have what it takes?" That's a legitimate question for anyone applying for a responsible position. College presidents, coaches of professional teams, CEOs of large companies, and people in high public office are scrutinized carefully to determine whether or not they have what it takes to do the job. Are they educated and trained for what they are aspiring to do? Do they have an admirable résumé that reflects sufficient experience and a successful track record? What about references? Are they respected by their peers, and do others think highly of their qualifications? These are serious and important questions with regard to the aspiring leader.

Now let's up the stakes and ask a more profound question: Do you have what it takes to rule the world? Now I realize that this question isn't appropriate for most people, but it is a legitimate question to ask any person seeking a position of global leadership. Think for a moment about some of the examples of history. Alexander the Great thought he could rule the world, but he died as a drunkard in Babylon at a young age. Napoleon had delusions of grandeur too, but he ended up incarcerated on an island by those whom he attempted to rule. And what about Hitler? His egomaniacal tyranny of Europe ended in disaster. Over the centuries there has been no lack of effort by individuals seeking to become number one in the world. Yet no one has been able to demonstrate that he or she has what it takes.

In contrast to these paltry attempts at global leadership, the prophet Isaiah predicted that a Child would be born who would have the divine qualifications to become the ultimate ruler. In fact, he said that His name would be called "Mighty God" (9:6). Gospel writers of the New Testament identified this Person as Jesus Christ, the Son of God (John 20:31). So let's go back and consider Isaiah's prophecy again:

> 6 For a child will be born to us, a son will be given to us;
> And the government will rest on His shoulders;
> And His name will be called Wonderful Counselor,
> Mighty God,
> Eternal Father, Prince of Peace.
> 7 There will be no end to the increase of
> His government or of peace,
> On the throne of David and over his kingdom,
> To establish it and to uphold it with justice and righteousness
> From then on and forevermore.
> The zeal of the Lord of hosts will accomplish this.
> ISAIAH 9:6-7

Currently there is much talk about global governance and a New World Order. The thought seems to be that if the nations of the world can be brought under a single governing authority, then the world would at last discover universal peace. It's a nice idea, but history has proved that it won't work, and the Bible predicts its failure. Man cannot govern the world. He does not have what it takes.

A number of years ago, in January 1991, the New World Order was a hot topic in the context of Operation Desert Storm in Iraq. Former President George Bush, Sr. was popularizing the subject, and people were wondering exactly what he meant. About that time a man from Merritt Island, Florida, sent a letter to the editor of the *Orlando Sentinel* on the subject of the New World Order. Here's what he wrote:

THERE IS MUCH speculation about what President Bush means when he speaks of a *"New World Order."* Perhaps I can help clarify the phrase for your readers.

"New World Order" refers to the coming *world* government. National boundaries and elections will be unnecessary under this *new* government, because we will be governed by an international elite. Our *new* leaders will be like Plato's "philosopher kings." Of course, this will include men like George Bush, Mikhail Gorbachev and Yitzhak Shamir.

All the needs of the simple folk (you and me) will be provided for. We will spend most of our time on some sunlit hillside. It will be covered with the lilies of the field, daisies, poppies and other flowers. We will all clasp hands; men and women; blacks, yellows, whites and polka dots; and we will collectively gaze into space. Then we will sing in harmony about brotherhood and Coca-Cola.

Of course, should any of us sing off-key, our benevolent rulers will send men armed with axe handles to club us into conformity.[1]

It's quite obvious that this man saw the irony in the phrase "our benevolent rulers," probably because of the lessons of history. That was the way of Fascism and Communism, and according to Bible prophecy that will also be the way of the global rule of Antichrist (Rev. 13). There is an inherent selfishness and lust for power in the governments of men that automatically sets them up for failure.

The principle that power corrupts and absolute power corrupts absolutely has been proved over and over in the history of the world. And therein lies the dilemma, for authority and power are essential elements of government. Yet man's authority is a corruptible authority because man is a sinful being. That is why if there is ever to be a government that is truly equitable, truly just, and truly unselfish, it must be a government established by God, for God is the only Person in the universe who is perfectly righteous, totally just, and purely unselfish.

The point here is that a new world order is exactly what Isaiah is talking about in Isaiah 9:6-7. What he has in view, however, is not a new world based on human government. He is speaking of a new world founded on the principles of *divine* government. In fact, he says that the name of the Person who will rule the world in that day is "Mighty God." This Person is the one benevolent ruler who has the character, ability, and resources to bring peace and prosperity to our beleaguered planet.

So let's continue our patient study of Isaiah's special prophecy concerning the Child born and the Son given, on whose shoulder the government will rest. Isaiah tells us in verse 6 that His name will be called Mighty God. As in English, that name is two words in the Hebrew text—"*El*," the word for God, and *gibbor*, the Hebrew word for might and power. So *El Gibbor* literally means "God who is mighty," or "Mighty God."

We have already seen in previous chapters that the Bible identifies this Person as Jesus Christ. So let's consider what this name means concerning Him.

JESUS CHRIST, AS GOD, HAS SUPREME AUTHORITY

The first thing I'd like you to notice as we focus our attention on the first of the two words in the compound name *El Gibbor* is that *El* is the shortened form of *Elohim*, the name of the God of Creation. The first time God is mentioned in the Bible, it is by this name *Elohim*: "In the beginning God [*Elohim*] created the heavens and the earth" (Gen. 1:1). In other words *Elohim* is the God of heaven who created all things; and *El* is the shortened form of that name.

Most of us have shortened forms of our names. For example, people call me Dan even though my official name is Daniel. I use the longer form of my name when signing documents or important papers, but normally I am just Dan (that is, except for my mother who called me Danny). Well, in similar fashion *Elohim* in the Bible is often referred to as simply *El*.

Now as we begin our study of this designation of our Lord's name, I need to inform you that this verse is a problem to many people who have chosen not to acknowledge that Jesus Christ is God. It is a problem to liberal churchmen as well as to most of the sects and cults. It is a problem to all other religions of the world, and clearly it is a problem to atheists and agnostics. The reason, of course, is that the Person of Isaiah's prophecy, whom the Bible identifies as Jesus, is said to be Mighty God—the very God who created the universe.

So let's think for a moment about the arguments of the critics against this verse in their attempts to diminish the claim to deity for this Child.

Arguments of the Critics

1. THE CULTS—ONLY A GOD

When the cults come to this name in Isaiah 9:6, they try to diminish its force by saying that this person will only be *a* god— "a mighty god." By this they mean that he will be one god among many, like the gods of the Greek Pantheon; or that he will be a little god who is subservient to *the* God. They make a big point of the fact that there is no article *the* with this name; and so they think they have the grammatical right to supply the indefinite article *a*.

The problem with this is that they are grammatically incorrect. There is no indefinite article in the Hebrew language. Rather, the point of the *anarthrous* construction (where the article *the* is not used) is to emphasize the *quality* or *character* of what is being referenced. In the third chapter of this book I explained in detail this grammatical phenomenon of the Hebrew language (as well as of the Greek language), especially as it is misunderstood by the Jehovah's Witnesses. Here I simply want to reaffirm what I said there: The name Mighty God is actually a strong assertion that this Person would be God Almighty! So you see, when the cults use this fallacious understanding of the lack of the article *the* in the Hebrew text, they are either expressing their ignorance or they are being deliberately deceptive. The grammar argues for the full force of "Mighty God" as applied to this Person. It is important to understand that.

2. LIBERAL CHURCHMEN—A "GODLIKE" PERSON OR "HERO"

Liberal churchmen don't like to admit the deity of Jesus either. They see Him simply as a good man who was a martyr for the cause of what is right. They will say many good things about Jesus, but they do not want Him to be God. Thus they translate Isaiah 9:6 to say that the Child will be a "godlike" person or someone to be admired. John Martin, in *The Bible Knowledge Commentary*, refers to this argument of the liberals when he says that some have suggested that this simply means a "godlike person or a hero."[2]

Now according to theological liberals, this understanding of Christ as a godlike person goes back to Genesis 3, where we read that Satan tempted Eve in the Garden of Eden. Satan told Eve on that occasion that if she disobeyed God and ate of the tree of the knowledge of good and evil, she would not die as God had said she would. He convinced her that God was trying to keep her from becoming like Himself. Satan put it this way: "For God knows that in the day you eat from it your eyes will be opened, and you will be like God, knowing good and evil" (Gen. 3:5). The word "God" in this verse is the word *Elohim*.

So jumping forward in history to Isaiah 9, the liberal idea is to say that Jesus was not truly God. Rather, like Eve, he became godlike through his achievements and exalted knowledge. By the way, this is what the Mormons teach, and it is a major tenet of New Age thinking also. We all can become godlike, they insist, just like Jesus did, and just like the mystic gurus do. All we need to do is pursue the course of divine enlightenment as Eve did when she ate of the tree of the knowledge of good and evil.

There is one further argument that liberals make in this regard. They appeal to the *gibbor* portion of the name *El Gibbor*, noticing that it is sometimes translated as "hero" or "warrior" and even "leader." The primary meaning of *gibbor*, however, is "to be strong or mighty, even powerful and valiant"; but they prefer the idea that the word means simply "hero." This allows them to see Christ as merely a godlike person who was heroic—a godlike hero who fought and conquered like an invincible god (after the likeness of Hercules, who became a god through his amazing achievements in battle).

So here's the deal: The error of liberal theologians, Mormons, or New Age religionists is that they believe any person can become godlike and heroic just like Isaiah predicted Jesus would. They believe we can all become *El Gibbor*; we can all become Mighty God. In all of this they are attempting to make *El* mean something less than the personal, eternal, infinite Creator-God of heaven. So how do we answer that?

The Answer of the Bible

1. ISAIAH'S PERSPECTIVE ON *EL*

When seeking to understand words, it is always important to observe who is using them. In the final analysis it really doesn't matter what the cultists think about what Isaiah said or what the liberals believe. What is important in the matter of communication is what Isaiah meant by these terms when he used them. So it would be prudent to examine other passages in Isaiah where the prophet used the term *El*.

(1) Isaiah 7:14—"El" is God with us.

We have looked at this verse on numerous occasions in this study because it has a great bearing on Isaiah 9:6-7. Here I simply want to concentrate on the name Immanuel: "Behold, a virgin will be with child and bear a son, and she will call His name Immanuel." *Immanuel*, you will recall, means "God with us" in Hebrew. This is, in fact, what Matthew says in the birth account of Jesus: "'. . . IMMANUEL,' which translated means, 'GOD WITH US'" (Matt. 1:23). Before Isaiah ever gets to chapter 9, verse 6, he tells us in 7:14 that there will be a Child born to a virgin whose name would be "God [*El*] with us."

Now there are a couple of important things to notice regarding Isaiah's use of *El*. First, Isaiah is stating that the Child will be "God with us" from birth. This is totally different from the New Age, liberal, and cultist perspective that the child would become a god by His achievements. Isaiah boldly affirmed that the Child would be "God with us" from the moment of His birth. It's an entirely different concept.

Second, there is a great reversal here. This verse is not referring to a man who will become a god; conversely, it relates the fact that God will become a man. Think about it! This is amazing. It is absolutely unique. It's totally different from anything being suggested by the religions of the world. Other religions want us to believe that man can become a god, but the Scriptures reveal that it is quite the opposite with Jesus. He is the Creator-God, *Elohim*, who became a man in order to save us from our sins. In the mind of Isaiah, *El* is the God of heaven who will be "with us."

(2) Isaiah 31:3—"El" is not a man.

Isaiah tells the Israelites in this text that their help is in God and not in the nations around them, especially not in Egypt. He says, "Now the Egyptians are men, and not God, And their horses are flesh and not spirit; so the LORD will stretch out His hand, and he who helps will stumble and he who is helped will fall, and all of them will come to an end together." This verse is saying that the Lord alone is supreme, and that everyone else— the helpers and the ones who are helped—are going to fall.

The Egyptians are described here as "men," which is the translation of the Hebrew word *adam*. In Genesis we learn that the first man was called Adam (the Hebrew term for man or mankind). So this is what the Egyptians are in contrast to God, according to Isaiah. The word for "God" in this verse is again the shortened form *El*, the point being that Egyptians are *adam* (man), not *El* (God). Isaiah is conscious of the antithesis between the two words and is making a significant distinction. Either you are *adam* or you are *El*—one or the other. And if you are *adam*, then you cannot be at the same time *El*. God and man are distinct and separate. You see, *El* in the mind of Isaiah is the great *Elohim* of creation. *El* cannot be mere man seeking to become godlike. *El* is truly God Himself!

(3) Isaiah 10:21—El Gibbor is a name for God in Isaiah.

In this verse Isaiah is speaking of the remnant that will one day return to the land of Israel out of captivity in Babylon: "A remnant will return," writes the prophet, "the remnant of Jacob, to the mighty God" (*El Gibbor*). Then he continues, "For though your people, O Israel, may be like the sand of the sea, *only* a remnant within them will return" (v. 22). Now think of this for a moment. To whom will the remnant return? Isaiah tells us that it will be to Mighty God (*El Gibbor*). These are the exact two words found in Isaiah 9:6 just one chapter earlier. Here in Isaiah 10, he is speaking of *the very God of Israel*, the true God of heaven and earth. This is clearly the One to whom the remnant will return. Isaiah demonstrates to us that *El Gibbor* is a name for God Himself and cannot be a mere description of a godlike hero.

2. THE OLD TESTAMENT PERSPECTIVE ON "*EL*"

If we step back to look at the broader perspective of the Old Testament, we see that Moses, Nehemiah, and Jeremiah have the same understanding of *El Gibbor* as that of Isaiah. *El Gibbor*, or Mighty God, is always the one true God of Heaven.

(1) Deuteronomy 10:17—Moses

Notice how Moses reflects his understanding of God: "For the LORD your God [*El*] is the God of gods and the Lord of lords, the great, the mighty [*gibbor*], and the awesome God. . . ." Moses understands God (*El*) to be great (*gibbor*). In other words, He is *El Gibbor*, Mighty God. Now what God is he referring to? Is it a human person who has become a spiritual hero? No, not at all! It is the very God of Heaven—the "God of gods." Moses understands that the two words *El Gibbor* do go together as a fitting name for the God of Abraham, Isaac, and Jacob.

(2) Nehemiah 9:32—Nehemiah

We see the same emphasis in the writings of Nehemiah, who seems to be quoting Moses. He says, "Now therefore, our God [*El*], the great, the mighty [*gibbor*], and the awesome God, who dost keep covenant and loving-kindness. . . ." Again, we see that Nehemiah is referring to the one supreme God spoken of in the Scriptures. This God (*El*), according to Nehemiah, is mighty (*gibbor*). He too sees *El Gibbor* as the awesome God of creation (9:6).

(3) Jeremiah 32:18—Jeremiah

Moses (as quoted by Nehemiah) wrote prior to the days of Isaiah, but Jeremiah wrote a century later than Isaiah, describing the very things that Isaiah predicted. In Jeremiah 32:18 he exclaims, ". . . O great and mighty God [*El Gibbor*]. The LORD of hosts is His name." So who is Jeremiah referring to in this great exclamation? The previous verse tells us of whom he is speaking: "Ah Lord GOD! Behold, Thou hast made the heavens and the earth by Thy great power and by Thine outstretched arm! Nothing is too difficult for Thee" (v. 17). Who is this Mighty God (*El Gibbor*), according to Jeremiah? It is the God of Creation—the God of heaven and earth.

Putting It All Together

Let's summarize what we have been discussing in response to the inadequate view of the cultists and liberals. First, *El Gibbor* is a normative name for God in the Bible—it is used by Moses, by Nehemiah, and by Jeremiah. Second, *El Gibbor* is the way Isaiah describes God in the context of his book. *El Gibbor* is the Mighty God of Heaven, the Creator of the Universe. The critics of Isaiah's prophecy have no leg to stand on. Their arguments are mere wisps of imagination floating in the breeze of igno-rance. A patient study of Scripture shows that Isaiah meant what he said—the Child-Son would be Mighty God.

This is why F. C. Jennings, when referring to the name Mighty God in Isaiah 9:6, wrote in his commentary, "It is as sim-ple, clear, unequivocal a claim of supreme deity for Messiah as could be expressed in human language."[3]

Now the crux of the matter is this: Isaiah is saying that the Child-Son Messiah, on whose shoulder the government will rest, of whose Kingdom and peace there will be no end, who will bring justice and righteousness to the earth, *is none other than the El Gibbor of Scripture*. He is the Mighty God. And because He is Mighty God, He has supreme authority to accomplish His purpose. He will inaugurate a new world order of His choosing and in His time. As Isaiah concluded, "The zeal of the LORD of hosts will accomplish this" (9:7).

JESUS CHRIST, AS GOD, HAS INFINITE RESOURCES

Perhaps you remember that I began this chapter by asking the question, Do you have what it takes to do the job? Well, when we consider that Jesus Christ, the Child of Isaiah's prophecy, is Mighty God (7:14; 9:6-7), we begin to realize that He really does have what it takes to rule the world and establish a kingdom of justice and righteousness. As God, He has infinite resources to fix what is wrong and to return Planet Earth to the way God intended for it to be.

In the name *El Gibbor*, *gibbor* means that He is resourceful and powerful—He is almighty to do what needs to be done. Now ponder this: It is one thing to say that you are going to do something, but quite another to have the ability and resources to actually accomplish it.

Previous rulers who have aspired to global rule have all demonstrated their inability to close the deal. They are dead and buried, and the world has gone on without them. Of course, new governments have replaced the old, but in one way or another the new ones also have their own deficiencies and shortcomings. It is (and will continue to be) a mad cycle of inadequacy and limitations of man-made governments. The Bible says that the final form of this madness—when Satan tries to finally achieve global supremacy through his ultimate ruler (whom we call the Antichrist)—will end in failure as well.

There is good news, however! The government of Jesus Christ will not be like the government of men because Jesus is almighty. This is reflected in the term *El Gibbor*. As *El Gibbor*, Jesus is omnipotent, which means that His power is infinite. There is absolutely nothing that He cannot do, and nothing that His power cannot accomplish. Pin that thought up on the bulletin board of your mind. *There is nothing He cannot do!* In Jeremiah 32:27 God asks the question, ". . . is anything too difficult for Me?" It is a rhetorical question with an obvious answer: "No! There is nothing too difficult for You!" (cf. Jer. 32:17).

In the setting of these verses in Isaiah 9, this attribute of the Messiah is essential. Establishing a just and righteous government in our sin-polluted world will require divine ability. There are the environmental concerns of our worn-out and abused planet as well—everything from increased ozone levels to incredible pollution of the earth's natural resources. Only God can fix all of that. In addition, according to Isaiah, natural dangers that cause brevity of life will be greatly diminished in the Kingdom Age (Isa. 11:6-9; 65:17-23, esp. v. 20). Now in anticipation of the fulfillment of this prophecy, Jesus Christ has already demonstrated His ability to heal the sick, cure the deformed, and rebuke the weather. The Child of Isaiah's prophecy is Jesus

Christ, and He will do all of these things in the future Kingdom. He will be equal to the task because He is Almighty God.

In a personal sense, however, this may all seem like a tease. You may be thinking, *Well, if Jesus is Mighty God, why doesn't He do a miracle for me? Why doesn't He step into my messed-up life and solve my problems? Why doesn't He give me a little more money? Why doesn't He solve my relational difficulties? Why doesn't God, if He's mighty, exercise that might on my behalf?*

Well, part of the answer to those questions is to bear in mind that the name Mighty God is the second of four couplets, all of which are a single unit. It is one name, remember? We cannot isolate Mighty God from the first thing that is mentioned—that He is the Counseling Wonder. Therefore we have to go to Him and ask, "Lord, is it Your good counsel to intervene on my behalf, or is there some other purpose that You are working out in my life by allowing this to continue?"

You see, our God is not only mighty, He is also wise. Can He do a miracle on your behalf and solve every problem you have right now? Absolutely He can! Will He do it? Not necessarily. With God there is always a bigger picture, and a miracle may not be the best course of action for you and those around you. Yet there is one thing we can assume with confidence: If He doesn't do something spectacular, when He very well could if He wished, then there is something better going on. Christ is almighty—there is no question about that. But He will never use His might contrary to His wisdom.

Now what is true of the fact that Christ is a Counseling Wonder is also true concerning the other parts of His name. As Father of Eternity, He is more concerned about our spiritual development than about solving our present social and financial dilemmas. In fact, those problems may be the very things that

He is using to forge our character to make us into a person of integrity by increasing the depth of our faith (Jas. 1:2-4). We cannot forget that He is also the Prince of Peace. The one thing He has promised to do is to give us supernatural inner peace in the midst of external turmoil (Phil. 4:6-7). That, in fact, may be the greater demonstration of His might. Miracles in the spiritual dimension of life are always greater than miracles in the physical realm (Matt. 9:1-8). So you see, we need to view Mighty God in the perspective of all that He is.

As we probe the infinite resources of the Messiah as reflected in the word *gibbor* or mighty, let's consider a few examples to expand our understanding of what He can do.

(1) As God, He created *the world.*

No doubt the first thing that comes to mind when thinking of the almighty nature of God is His creative ability. In many of the texts we have considered in this chapter, that is what the name Mighty God reflected: He created the heavens and the earth. If we want to see might in action, we should go to Genesis 1 and read the account of creation. *Elohim* simply spoke the word, and the world came into being. He uttered a command, and the universe spun in the palm of His hand. With His fingers He carved the valleys and molded the mountains. Living beings were crafted by His artistry, and then He breathed into them the breath of life. He is the source of all energy, and the universe quivers at His voice because He is the Almighty Creator.

In the New Testament all of this is attributed to Christ. John tells us that nothing was created apart from His involvement (John 1:3). Paul was very specific when He said of Jesus, "For by him were all things created, that are in heaven, and that are in earth, visible and invisible, whether *they be* thrones, or dominions, or principalities, or powers: all things were created by him, and for him" (Col. 1:16, KJV). Isaiah predicted that the virgin-born Child would be *Elohim* among us, and the New Testament verifies that Jesus was that Person. As Mighty God, He is the Creator.

But God is not creating today—at least in the sense that He did in Genesis 1—right? So how does He manifest His power today? Let's step back and watch what He does for a moment. Consider a brief quote from Horatius Bonar as he reflects on the way God works in our contemporary world:

> When man proceeds to the accomplishment of some mighty enterprise, he puts forth prodigious efforts, as if by the sound of his axes and hammers he would proclaim his own fancied might, and bear down opposing obstacles. He cannot work without sweat, and dust, and noise. When God would do a marvellous work, such as may amaze all heaven and earth, He commands silence all around, sends forth the still small voice, and then sets some feeble instrument to work, and straightway it is done! Man toils and pants, and after all effects but little: the Creator, in the silent majesty of power, noiseless yet resistless, achieves by a word the infinite wonders of omnipotence!

And then he gives an illustration:

> In order to loose the bands of winter, and bring in the verdure of the pleasant spring, He does not send forth His angels to hew in pieces the thickened ice, or to strip off from the mountain's side the gathered snows, or to plant anew over the face of the bleak earth, flowers fresh from His creating hand. No! He breathes from His lips a mild warmth into the frozen air; and forthwith, in stillness but in irresistible power, the work proceeds; the ice is shivered, the snows dissolve, the rivers resume their flow, the earth awakes as out of sleep, the hills and the valleys put on their freshening verdure, the fragrance of earth

takes wing and fills the air, till a new world of beauty rises in silence amid the dissolution of the old!

Such is God's method of working, both in the natural and in the spiritual world—silent, simple, majestic and resistless![4]

That is how God works in the world today. He manifests His power in the processes that He put in place when creating the universe. Can God create a full-grown tree overnight? Of course. It is never a question of His ability. Is that how He normally does things? Well, no. The normal procedure is for man to plant a seed, then water and cultivate it over a period of time, and eventually the seedling turns into a mighty oak or whatever. That's how God does it—and that is no less a manifestation of God's might than if He had called it into being on the spot. Sowing and reaping is how the mighty God works.

Life works that way as well. Occasionally God dips into life and does something phenomenal, but that is the exception to the rule. Usually He expects us to pay attention to the process of sowing and reaping. Listen to the apostle Paul:

> *Do not be deceived, God is not mocked; for whatever a man sows, this he will also reap. For the one who sows to his own flesh shall from the flesh reap corruption, but the one who sows to the Spirit shall from the Spirit reap eternal life. And let us not lose heart in doing good, for in due time we shall reap if we do not grow weary.*
>
> —GALATIANS 6:7-9

Our God works in the still, small ways of life as we obey Him and acknowledge His wisdom in our affairs. Then in the process, day after day, month after month, year after year, He builds a mighty oak—and it is a miracle of His omnipotence. So don't become critical of God if He does not come through with a special miracle for you on the spot. Just exercise patience, and let God do things His way.

(2) As God, He redeemed *the world.*

As I mentioned earlier, redemption is by far the most impressive demonstration of God's might. Jesus Christ is *El Gibbor* in creation, but He's also *El Gibbor* in redemption. What goes on in the realm of spiritual things greatly outweighs that which happens in the realm of physical things. Consider the following comparison:

When King David was writing the poetry that became psalms in the Psalter, he reflected on God's work of creation with these words: "When I consider Thy heavens, the work of *Thy fingers,* the moon and the stars, which Thou hast ordained . . ." (Ps. 8:3, emphasis mine). Isn't that amazing! David saw creation as merely the finger-work of God! Contrast that with Isaiah's description of redemption in Isaiah 53. In that passage we are face-to-face with the Messiah as He dies for the sins of the world, as He bears our sorrows and carries our griefs, as He is bruised for our iniquities, with the chastisement for our peace upon Him. Isaiah introduces all of this suffering by saying, "And to whom has *the arm* of the LORD been revealed?" (v. 1, emphasis mine). Here is the point: When God created the universe, it was mere finger-work. But when He died on the cross for our sins, He had to roll up His sleeves. Creation took place as God spoke a word, but when He redeemed the world, great agony and suffering were required. Christ's work as our Redeemer was a more impressive display of His power than was His work as Creator.

Understanding this fact will readjust our priorities. From the perspective of God, spiritual things are always more important than physical things; but we in our ignorance tend to think just the opposite. One of our biggest problems is that we major in minors and minor in majors. We have a wrong sense of values and priorities because we don't see things as God sees them. Isaiah understood this when he shared God's words to us: "'For My thoughts are not your thoughts, neither are your ways My ways,' declares the LORD. 'For *as* the heavens are higher than the earth, so are My ways higher than your ways, and My thoughts than your thoughts'" (Isa. 55:8-9). You see, we just don't think like God does. We major in physical and temporal things, but He majors in spiritual and eternal things. And so we misunderstand God when He doesn't do a miracle to bail us out of a jam. Most likely He is doing something of spiritual importance, and a miracle would mess that up.

In the hard times of life we need to remember this: God did His greatest miracle when He saved us from our sins. Reflecting on that should fill our hearts with a genuine sense of gratitude, even when things are not going well. The rest of the time it's a matter of sowing and reaping. Do what is right, trust the Lord, be patient, and He will show you that He is Mighty God as He builds a great tree out of your life (see Ps. 1:1-3).

(3) As God, He governs *the world.*

One day Christ will come back to earth and inaugurate His Kingdom as Isaiah has predicted. At that time the government will be upon His shoulder, and there will be worldwide peace. Also, justice and righteousness will prevail, and God's original purpose for creation will be restored. At that time He will fix what is broken and heal what is hurt. We all yearn for that day to come, and one day it will.

In the meantime God is still sovereign in the affairs of the world. Things may look out of control, and evil may appear to be winning, but that does not nullify the fact that God is still working all things toward a predetermined end. The Kingdom *will* come, and Messiah *will* rule. God's plan for the ages is still on course, and "the zeal of the LORD of hosts will accomplish this" (Isa. 9:7).

Now all of this means that God is the ultimate ruler of the world. Always! Man may appear to be ruling from time to time, and human rulers will continue to come and go, but their rule is just an illusion of power, for ultimate authority is with God. That is the way it has always been, and that is the way it will always be. And the exciting truth is that those who acknowledge His authority now will be those who reign with Him in the Kingdom (2 Tim. 2:12; Rev. 3:21).

After Christ's resurrection from the dead, and prior to His ascension into heaven, He made this claim to His followers: "All authority has been given to Me in heaven and on earth" (Matt. 28:18). Rest assured, Christ will not receive His authority at the time of the future Kingdom—the authority is already His! Therefore those who are wise submit to His authority now. He created us, He redeemed us, and now He has the right to rule us. That's the sequence Paul was thinking of when he wrote, ". . . do you not know that your body is a temple of the Holy Spirit who is in you, whom you have from God, and that you are not your own? For you have been bought with a price: therefore glorify God in your body" (1 Cor. 6:19-20).

Christ's governance is not just a future event when He will rule the world from the throne of David. His authority is pervasive in the universe, and it is in effect in the here and now. He is Mighty God *now*; and that means that He is the Lord of life now.

If you are attempting to rule over your own life, why not submit to Him at this moment and acknowledge His lordship over your life? It is the only wise thing to do, and it's the only way to experience kingdom living in your heart. Remember the old adage: If He is not Lord of all, He is not your Lord at all. He is Mighty God! And understanding that is the answer to life.

HERE'S THE BOTTOM LINE

1. *Only Jesus Can Bring a New World Order*

Here is the essence of *hope*. Christ alone has the authority and ultimate resources to fix what's wrong with our world. Any attempt by men to do this will simply be another form of the old world order (even if they have the presumption to call it a *"New World Order"*). So as you listen to all of the hype about trying to bring something new to our planet, realize in your heart that nothing new will ever really happen until Jesus comes back. Place your hope firmly in Him, and anticipate His coming. The Person who is Mighty God is the only answer to the troubles of our world.

2. *Only Jesus Can Make Sense out of Your Life*

Here is the essence of *faith*. Trusting Christ as your Savior from sin and acknowledging Him as the Lord of your life is the only way to know the spiritual dimensions of the Kingdom in your heart. You can know His peace now, and you can experience righteous living now. It all depends on who is ruling in your life.

If you are trying to govern yourself, you will have no more success than those who try to govern the world. The reason, of course, is that your heart is selfish in the same way as theirs. If you buy into the existential culture and try to grab all the gusto you can get because you're worth it, you will end up disillusioned and unfulfilled. If all of your aspirations for life are focused on yourself, and you keep asking God to fit into your plans, then I can assure you that you will never end up where you want to be. Self-rule is always doomed from the beginning and is destined for failure.

The alternative is to trust Christ as the Mighty God of your life. Sow to the Spirit as He counsels you to do in His Word; then you will reap the benefits of life. Let spiritual and eternal things be the major focus of your heart and mind, and you will observe the real power of His works. Ask Him what He sees and how you can fit into His plans, instead of telling Him what you see and how you want Him to fit into your plans. Acknowledge His lordship and depend upon His strength. Then, and only then, will you discover that He is *El Gibbor*— He is Mighty God!

6

THE MASTER OF THE KEYS

Opening the Door to Tomorrow and Beyond

". . . Eternal Father . . ."

ISAIAH 9:6

When entering unfamiliar territory it is always helpful to have a guide. Knowing which path to take and what pitfalls to avoid is essential to reaching the destination safely. A guide who knows the way is invaluable in those situations.

Over the years my wife, Karilee, and I have led many tours to Israel and other lands of the Bible. In each country, whether Egypt or Jordan or Greece or Israel, we always hired a guide who was a native of the area. These guides always knew the best way to go and the best time to arrive at a destination. If there was ever a problem, they were the buffer between the situation and our group, because they knew both the language and the culture. Although I knew the biblical significance of the sites that we visited, I learned to depend upon the expert oversight and advice of these professional guides. There was a sense of safety and well-being in simply knowing that they were there and acting on our behalf. One particular guide, Amos, even became a close friend, and we would ask for him upon each return trip.

I begin this way because we are all facing unfamiliar territory, and we all need a guide. None of us have experienced death, and no one reading this book has yet crossed over into heaven. It is true that Jesus Christ knows the way through death into the abode of God, but apart from Him we are lost. As Thomas once said to Jesus, "Lord, we do not know where You are going; how do we know the way?" Jesus answered, "I am the way" (John 14:5-6). You see, we are in desperate need of a guide—someone who knows the narrow way and can safely lead us where we have never been. Jesus is that guide, and that is the significance of Isaiah's third couplet, Eternal Father (Isa. 9:6).

Before looking more closely into the meaning of this name, however, I want to remind you that not everyone recognizes the importance of depending upon Jesus as their spiritual guide. In fact, false guides have duped many unsuspecting travelers into thinking they know the way when in fact they don't. Because Jesus is the unique Savior, every other religious perspective is a false hope. Yet there is one particular deviant path that illustrates the deceptive nature of the false guides more than the others. And that is the spirit guides of the New Age phenomenon.

NEW AGE SPIRIT GUIDES

There is a New Age practice known as channeling in which individuals seek personal contact with spirit beings. These entities are called spirit guides, and the purpose of contacting them is to receive counsel on life and eternal existence. No doubt there are many fakes, but for the most part this practice appears to be a real involvement with the spirit world. In a typical channeling experience a man or a woman offers himself or herself as a medium of communication through which a controlling spirit will speak with a different voice through that channeler. Biblically speaking, this practice is very much like classic demon possession.

I do not profess to be an expert on this phenomenon, but for the last thirty years it's been a major aspect of the New Age Movement. Tal Brooke of the Spiritual Counterfeits Project writes about channeling in his book *When the World Will Be as One*, an early exposé of the New Age Movement. In a chapter entitled "Contact" he mentions Jane Roberts from Elmira, New York, who channels a spirit called Seth. Then he proceeds to describe similar experiences:

> . . . newer channels have come on the scene . . . [spirit guides] such as "Ramtha" [channeled by J.Z. Knight, a lady] and "Lazaris" [channeled by Jach Pursel]—who feature among the bright new stars of Shirley MacLaine's autobiographies such as *Out on a Limb* and *Dancing in the Light.*
>
> Yet these newer entities have arrived with exquisite timing to a world in waiting. The advance work has been done. Unlike Seth, who only muttered in dark rooms before a handful of observers, Ramtha and Lazaris have spoken on live television before hundreds of millions of viewers. Both Ramtha and Lazaris have appeared on the Merv Griffin Show, the Phil Donahue Show, and the Oprah Winfrey Show, among others. And news teams such as ABC's 20/20 have done specials on these entities and their human channels. Compared to Seth, they have achieved superstar celebrity status.[1]

Tal Brooke goes on to talk about the popularity of these channelers and their spirit guides as reflected in the enormous fees people are willing to pay to see and hear them:

Time magazine's December 1987 cover story on the New Age Movement mentioned that the enormous gate fees of these entities and their channels comprised only one indicator of the surging popular interest. That month's *New Age Journal* featured channeling on its cover story and stated that J.Z. Knight, who channels Ramtha, "on an average weekend draws up to 700 participants at $400 apiece (280,000 dollars); she admits to earning millions of dollars from Ramtha."[2]

Another popular channeler is Jach Pursel who channels a spirit guide known as Lazaris. This is what Tal Brooke says about him:

When Jach Pursel, owner of the Illuminarium, tuned in on Lazaris, he had been a regional insurance supervisor in Florida and had started to dabble in meditation. On one of these occasions his wife addressed him and a different voice came through Jach. It was "Lazaris." The voice had a Chaucerian Middle English quality that has over the past 14 years "stayed impeccably consistent throughout thousands of hours of channeled talking, as has the personality supposedly doing the talking."[3]

New Age seekers are not interested in traditional religion, but they are interested in having contact with the spirit world. They are enthralled with spirit guides who will counsel them on life and supposedly lead them into eternal ecstasy. New Agers seem to realize that they are in uncharted waters as they face death and the life beyond; so they have turned to spirit guides to show them the way. Their popularity is indeed amazing. In 1998 Jon Klimo wrote the following in his psychological evaluation of the channeling experience:

Cases of channeling have become pervasive. An increasing number of people are now seeking and following the guidance provided through channeling. Accounts of the phenomenon have swept the media over the years. Dozens of new books said to be channeled are cropping up in bookstores. Millions of readers have been introduced to the phenomenon through actress Shirley MacLaine's best-selling books featuring her own dramatic, positive experiences with channels. All of this activity and visibility points to the fact that something very interesting and unusual is going on, and on a wide scale. Exactly *what* is going on, however, remains open to question.[4]

Unfortunately, New Agers have seen more reality in spirit channeling than they have seen in contemporary Christianity. Perhaps they and others like them who are seeking answers to life and death and the hereafter need to see us (Christians) a little more excited about the fact that in Christ we have something far more incredible than spirit guides and channeling.

You see, Jesus Christ is not just a spirit guide who speaks in unusual voices channeled through specially chosen people, nor is He merely a phantom that shows up occasionally via mystical experiences to only a few chosen initiates. Rather, He is actually God who took upon Himself human nature and lived among us. He is the One who died for us so that we might have our sins forgiven and have the hope of a future with God. He rose from the dead, demonstrating that He knows the way through death into eternal life. Furthermore, He comes by His Spirit to indwell all of us who put our trust in Him, for the purpose of guiding us in matters of life and death and beyond. What spirit guide of the New Age Movement could even begin to match these credentials? Jesus Christ is our unique and divine Spirit Guide.

What New Agers think they have in New Age channeling is

puny and pathetic, misleading and damning, compared to what we have in Jesus Christ. Jesus is the only legitimate Spirit Guide because He is the only guide who knows the way through death into the land of eternal happiness. He's been there and done that. No one else can make that claim, and no one else is Father of Eternity.

ANSWERING AN INITIAL QUESTION

How can the Son be called the Father? This particular aspect of our Lord's name (that He is Eternal Father) is perhaps the most difficult to understand. We realize that God is a triune God because the Scriptures present Him as Father and Son and Holy Spirit. But how, then, can Isaiah call the Son "Eternal Father"?

> *. . . and His name will be called Wonderful Counselor, Mighty God, Eternal Father, Prince of Peace.*
>
> —ISA. 9:6

Let me suggest three things to keep in mind as we seek to understand this special facet of His name.

1. The Son Is Not the Father

First of all, there is no article with this compound name. It is not *the* Eternal Father. We understand from previous studies that an *anarthrous* construction (where the article *the* is not used) places an emphasis on quality. Isaiah is emphasizing the idea that the Child has something about Him related to the quality of fatherliness.

I am like my father in many ways. He is with the Lord now, but people who knew him would often remark that many of my qualities are just like my father's. On a number of occasions I have had the opportunity to preach in my home church on Long

Island, where my dad was pastor for forty-nine years. After one particular sermon an elderly lady came up to me with glowing eyes and said, "Dan, you're the spitting image of your dad!" Now that was a wonderful compliment for me, and it is true that I preach like him and think like him in many ways. Yet although I share many of his qualities, I am distinct from him. I am not my father. In a similar way, Jesus can have many qualities of fatherliness without actually being *the* Father. There is no article with this name.

A second thing to notice is that in the Scriptures there is a clear distinction between Father and Son. In Psalm 2:2, for instance, the kings and judges of the earth are said to set themselves against *Jehovah and against His Anointed One.* Later in verse 7 the Anointed One is identified as the Son whom the Father (Jehovah) is going to enthrone as King of the earth. The Father and the Son are not the same here; they are distinct.

In the New Testament Jesus Christ is identified as the Son of God (John 20:31). Yet Jesus was constantly reminding us of the distinction between Him and the Father. We see this in the prayer of Gethsemane when Jesus prayed, "Father, if thou be willing, remove this cup from me: nevertheless not my will, but thine, be done" (Luke 22:42, KJV). It is obvious that there is a sharp distinction between the Father and the Son. This distinction, by the way, is something the Jehovah's Witnesses like to emphasize. They will say, "Don't you see? Jesus is not God because He talks to God." They correctly see the distinction between the two, but they are blind to the fundamental unity between the Father and the Son. We will consider this important issue in a moment.

One caution needs to be offered in this regard: Be very careful of the theological claim called "the Fatherhood of Christ." This is a teaching that says the Son *is* the Father. In this teaching the Son and the Father are *not just one in unity* within the plural Godhead, but Jesus is actually said to be the Father; so there is no Trinity. Isaiah 9:6 is one of the verses these people like to use to bolster this idea; yet that is not what Isaiah is saying. I had a friend who got caught in the web of this thinking, and he became very confused. The Fatherhood of Christ is not the way to solve the complications of explaining the tri-unity of God; it only compounds the problem. The Father and the Son are both God, but there is a clear and emphatic distinction between them. The Son is *not* the Father.

2. The Son Is One with the Father

The Bible not only emphasizes diversity in the Godhead, it also emphasizes unity. It is true that the Father and the Son are distinct—they are diverse. But it is also true that the Father and the Son are *one in essence*—they are one God. Granted, this is difficult to comprehend, but the reason for our difficulty is that we do not have a frame of reference for this concept within the realm of human experience. We can understand two, and we can understand one, but we cannot understand two (or three) that is also one. The tri-unity of God is one of the true mysteries of life.

So why do we believe in the tri-unity of God? The answer is simple: Because that's what the Bible teaches. It's a matter of biblical revelation, not a matter of reason. You see, the Bible clearly teaches that there is *one* God (Deut. 6:4—"The LORD our God *is* one LORD," KJV). At the same time, the Bible declares that Jesus is God. The same can be said for the Holy Spirit, whom the Bible presents as a distinct Person but who is nevertheless one with the Godhead. As a tri-unity God is unique, and that should not surprise us.

On the unity side, Jesus made many statements concerning

His complete oneness with the Father. In John 10:30, for instance, He said, "I and *my* Father are one" (KJV). Some have tried to say this means only that the Father and the Son are one in purpose, as you and I can be one in purpose with God. But that, again, is not what Jesus meant because He was speaking of essence, not purpose. The Jews understood it that way, for they picked up stones to stone Him for perceived blasphemy (v. 31—the very next verse). Jesus was claiming to be God, and they knew it.

Well, as we seek to answer the question, how can the Son be called the Father, we need to understand that the Son is truly one with the Father. We have seen that He is distinct from the Father, but we need to add that He is, nevertheless, one with the Father. This is why Jesus could say to Philip, "he that hath seen me hath seen the Father" (John 14:9, KJV).

3. The Son Performs a Fatherly Role

A final observation is that the Son performs a fatherly role, and that is the point of this couplet name, Eternal Father. Isaiah uses two Hebrew words here—*avi ad*—which literally means "Father of Eternity." In other words, the Son will perform the function of a father for those to whom He gives eternal life. He is not *the* Father of the Godhead, but He is *a* father to those who are His eternal children.

Now this is something we can readily understand. For instance, I personally am both a son and a father. A moment ago I told you about my father whom I tend to resemble in a number of ways. But I am also a father with two children, and my son also tends to resemble me. I am a son, but I am also a father. In the same way, the Son of God also performs the role of a father.

In the context of Isaiah 9, when the government is upon the

Son's shoulder, He will have the Father's authority to rule over the earth. As a father rules in his household, so the Son will be the father of the Kingdom. And when the world stands before the throne of God, the Son will have the Father's authority to judge all of mankind. This is what Jesus tells us in John 5:22: "For not even the Father judges anyone, but He has given all judgment to the Son." Jesus the Son will be the One to give eternal life to all whose names are written in the Book of Life, as a father giving privileges to his children. Jesus will be the Father of Eternity for all who enter eternity to enjoy it with Him. It is in this sense that Jesus is Eternal Father.

It is crucial that we understand this and apply it personally. Do you understand that only in Christ can you have the hope of eternal life? Do you know that He is the Father of Eternity and that as such, He is the only reliable Spirit Guide through the valley of death and into the wonderful eternal world where those who know Him will live with God forever? "And this is the record, that God hath given to us eternal life," John writes. Then he tells us how God gives us that eternal life: " . . . and this life is in his Son. He that hath the Son hath life; *and* he that hath not the Son of God hath not life. These things have I written unto you that believe on the name of the Son of God; that ye may know that ye have eternal life" (1 John 5:11-13, KJV).

This passage is saying what Isaiah is saying—Jesus is Father of Eternity. Only in Him can you have eternal life. So, have you placed your faith in Jesus Christ as the One who died for your sins, that in Him your sins might be forgiven and in Him you might receive eternal life? "But as many as received Him," says John 1:12, "to them He gave the right to become children of God, *even* to those who believe in His name."

So here are some things to remember as we begin to look more closely at this name: The Son is not the Father, but the Son is one with the Father, and the Son performs a fatherly role with regard to the Kingdom and with regard to eternal life.

FATHER (*AV*) IS A TERM OF ENDEARMENT

With that as an introduction to the study of this name, let's look at the two terms *Father* and *Eternal*. The first term in the Hebrew text is *Av*, the word for father. It's the initial syllable in the name *Ab*raham (*Av*-raham), "father of the people." So the name in Isaiah 9:6 is literally, "Father of Eternity."

When the question is asked, what will the Messiah be like? the answer according to Isaiah is, He will be like a father. But what does that really mean? Well, there are at least two things that a father does for his family: He provides security, and he provides guidance. Jesus Christ will provide both of these things for His people. In that way, He will be a father to them.

1. Jesus Christ Is Our Security

For a number of years my wife, Karilee, and I ministered at a four-seasons camp in northern Wisconsin. The camp was set on the southern boundary of the American Legion State Forest, and all of our horse trails and cross-country ski trails meandered through this wooded terrain. With forty thousand acres of virgin forest perched on the northern boundary of the camp, it became necessary for us on a regular basis to warn people of the dangers of wandering too far into the woods. It is easy to become disoriented in a heavily wooded environment, and the potential for getting lost was huge.

On one occasion a young boy turned up missing, and we all began searching for him. It was already late in the day, and darkness was coming on rapidly. As night settled on the forest, we were reduced to using flashlights as we scoured the woods looking for the boy. As providence would have it, it was the father who found him. The boy was sitting on a stump crying, with visions of bears and lions and tigers coming at him from all directions. When he saw the flashlight and realized it was his father, he jumped up and ran uncontrollably into the arms of his dad, who carried him to safety. In the days that followed, it was interesting to watch that little boy as he shadowed his father. They were inseparable. His father had come with the light to show him the way out of the darkness, and the boy knew better than he had ever known before that Dad was his security.

This is a picture of Israel in Isaiah 9. The nation was groping in awful darkness, and the people were weighed down with ignorance and sorrow in their sin. The land was bent down like a forest in the grip of a storm as the dread of foreign invasion petrified their hearts. The prophet predicted a day of gloom and anguish when suddenly out the midst of this darkness would burst a glorious light:

> *The people who walk in darkness*
> *Will see a great light;*
> *Those who live in a dark land,*
> *The light will shine on them.*
> *Thou shalt multiply the nation,*
> *Thou shalt increase their gladness;*
> *They will be glad in Thy presence*
> *As with the gladness of harvest,*
> *As men rejoice when they divide the spoil.*
> ISAIAH 9:2-3

The Messiah, like a father, will come with light to show His people the way out of the darkness. Isaiah portrays Him as their security and their hope. Now that's what the New Testament says Jesus is for us. We live in a morally dark world, and there is gloom and despair everywhere. But then Jesus steps into our impossible situation, and we hear Him say, "I am the light of the world; he who follows Me shall not walk in the darkness, but shall have the light of life" (John 8:12). What a glorious encouragement for those who are scared in the dark. Jesus is the light! Like a father coming with light to carry his child to safety, so Jesus comes with the light of the Gospel to carry all who trust Him to eternal safety. You see as *Av* ("Father"), He is our security.

> *More secure is no one ever*
> *Than the loved ones of the Savior;*
> *Not yon star on high abiding,*
> *Nor the bird in home-nest hiding.*[5]

2. Jesus Christ Is Our Guide

New Age channelers channel their spirit guides—satanic spirits, spirits of misinformation, spirits of deception, evil spirits masquerading as guides to truth. Listen, New Agers are desperate for spiritual guidance, and we have an answer for them that is truly out of this world. There is only one Spirit Guide who speaks the truth, and that is the "Son" of Isaiah's prophecy, who is also the Father of Eternity—none other than Jesus Christ.

You see, the New Testament teaches that when we receive Jesus Christ as our Savior, He comes to live within us by His Spirit. Now this is not the same as when a demon possesses a human channeler; but it is nevertheless true that the Holy Spirit comes to indwell us as the personal representative of Jesus Christ. This is something that every Christian needs to understand. Consider 1 John 3:24: "And we know by this that He [Jesus Christ] abides in us, by the Spirit which He has given us." In other words, we have direct contact with the spirit world because Jesus Christ indwells us by His Spirit.

Do you realize that as a Christian you are a vessel indwelt by the Spirit of God, so that it can be said that Christ actually inhabits you? He lives within you; that is a New Testament truth. Therefore, as a believer, if you have put your trust in Jesus Christ, if you are saved according to the Gospel, wherever you go Jesus Christ lives within you by His Spirit.

Now there are at least two practical consequences of this that apply to every Christian. First, the Spirit of God indwells every Christian for the purpose of giving spiritual guidance. This is different from the New Age phenomenon of channeling, where only special initiates are indwelt. We don't have to pay four hundred dollars per person to sit and listen to the spirit speaking through a special channeler. All of us have direct access to His spiritual guidance because He lives within each one of us. Speaking of genuine Christians, the apostle Paul writes, "For all who are being led by the Spirit of God, these are the sons of God" (Rom. 8:14). The Spirit of God gives us guidance.

It is also important to understand that His guidance is always according to truth. Jesus Himself made this clear: "But when He, the Spirit of truth, comes, He will guide you into all the truth" (John 16:13). Then Jesus went on to detail exactly what the Holy Spirit's mission would be: "He shall glorify Me," Jesus said, "for He shall take of Mine, and shall disclose *it* to you. All things that the Father has are Mine; therefore I said, that He takes of Mine, and will disclose *it* to you" (vv. 14-15).

How does He do that? Well, He does it through the Word of God, which is "the mind of Christ" (1 Cor. 2:16). God's Word is the truth (John 17:17), and in it He gives us our guidance. The mind of Christ is communicated to us through the study of His Word; and that is how the Holy Spirit enlightens our understanding. It was the Spirit who inspired the Word (2 Pet. 1:21), and it is the Spirit who helps us to understand it (John 16:13). That is how He guides us.

Now, there is a subjective side to the leading of the Spirit, when He speaks directly to our human spirit and impresses specific thoughts upon our minds. But these subjective impressions must always be brought under the direct authority of the Word of God so that we are not led astray by personal thoughts masquerading as spiritual thoughts. The Word of God is always our ultimate guide.

Which leads me to a question. New Agers will spend hundreds of dollars for a weekend to hear J. Z Knight channel Ramtha. What effort and expense are *you* willing to make to receive guidance and understanding from the Spirit of God through the study of His Word? Is your approach to Bible study superficial, simply carrying your Bible to church and then laying it back down again until next week? Or do you have an insatiable desire motivated by an inner compulsion to know as much of it as you can? Spiritual guidance is personally available for you, but you must make an effort in terms of time and energy to receive it.

A second application of this truth is that Christ wants each of us to become channels of His message of love to other people. That's right—you can become a channel for the Spirit of God to provide guidance for others. Not in the way that New Agers lose their identity and communicate in the strange voice of a spirit guide. Later they don't even remember what happened. In contrast, the Spirit of God works through our individual personalities and natural voices, in full awareness of the situation, to communicate the guidance of His Word. Notice how Paul describes the process:

Now all these things are from God, who reconciled us to Himself through Christ, and gave us the ministry of reconciliation. . . . Therefore, we are ambassadors for Christ, as

*though God were entreating through us; we beg you on
behalf of Christ, be reconciled to God.*

—2 CORINTHIANS 5:18, 20

So, there it is. Did you realize that you have been given that
privilege? The Holy Spirit who lives within you wants to speak
through you to impact other people with the Gospel of Christ.
You can channel the message from God so that others can be
blessed. What an incredible privilege!

CHANNELS ONLY
*How I praise Thee, precious Saviour,
That Thy love laid hold of me;
Thou hast saved and cleansed and filled me
That I might Thy channel be.
Channels only, blessed Master,
But with all Thy wondrous pow'r
Flowing thro' us, Thou canst use us
Every day and ev'ry hour.*[6]

This, then, is another aspect of *Av* ("Father") as it relates
to the Child of Isaiah's prophecy. As a father, He will give us
guidance.

ETERNITY (*AD*) IS A TERM OF HOPE

Visionaries who establish new entities such as companies, insti-
tutions, and even countries are often referred to as founding
fathers. George Washington is called the Father of the American
Republic because he was the first president of the United States.
Irenaeus, Polycarp, Origen, and others are called Church
Fathers, for they were foundational leaders of the early church.
Fathers start and establish new things, paving the way for oth-
ers who will follow.

In the same way, Jesus is the Father of Eternity for the human race. As the Son of God He came to earth as a virgin-born Child, and as a mature man He died for the sins of the world. Sin and alienation from God is mankind's greatest problem, and death is the damning consequence. By rising from the dead, Jesus was victorious over death and paved the way for all who put their trust in Him to also conquer death—not only physical death, but eternal death as well. That is the reason He can offer eternal life to all who believe in Him. Since He is the founder, establisher, and perpetual manager of eternal life for all human beings, Jesus is called the Father of Eternity.

We have been considering the first word *Av* ("Father") in Isaiah's third couplet name, Father of Eternity. The second word in the Hebrew text is "Eternity," which is the Hebrew word *ad*. This word is translated in the Bible by such words as duration, perpetuity, endurance, and forever. However, since this rendering (Father of Eternity) is different from the New American Standard Bible's "Eternal Father," and different from the KJV's and NIV's "Everlasting Father," let me explain why "Father of Eternity" is the better translation.

The first word *Av* ("Father") actually has an ending on it in the Hebrew text—*Avi*. The *i* part that is added to *Av* makes it a construct form according to Hebrew grammarians.[7] This simply means that "of" is added to the word "father," indicating that something else is going to follow. It is *father of* something—and that something is *Ad* ("Eternity"). So literally "Father" is the first word, "Eternity" is the second word, and "of" comes between them. It's not Eternal Father or Everlasting Father—it's Father *of* Eternity. That's precisely what the text is saying. The emphasis is on the fact that He has fatherly authority over eternal life.

Merrill F. Unger, the Hebrew scholar, in his commentary on

Isaiah said that the name Father of Eternity is "the Semitic idiom, 'where he who possesses a thing, etc. is called the father of it.'"[8] The Child-Son of Isaiah's prophecy possesses eternity; so He is the father of it. He is the Father of Eternity.

Let me share two observations in this regard. First, Jesus Christ is our entrance into eternity; and second, Jesus Christ is our enjoyment of eternity.

1. Jesus Christ Is Our Entrance into Eternity

Tickets or passes are often required for entrance into a special place or event. A person is excluded if he or she does not have the required pass. That's a common scenario in our society. Well, eternal life with God is like that. There is an entrance requirement, and unless a person meets that requirement, entrance is prohibited. Jesus Christ is that requirement, and knowing Him as personal Savior is the entrance pass into the enjoyment of eternal life. Eternal life is not an option apart from Jesus.

This is the clear teaching of the Bible. In Revelation 1:17-18 the victorious, resurrected, exalted Christ said, "Do not be afraid; I am the first and the last, and the living One; and I was dead, and behold, I am alive forevermore, and I have the keys of death and of Hades." So, who has the keys to unlock the bars of death and free a prisoner from the dungeon of Hades? It is Jesus Christ. He is the Master of the keys, and no one can experience freedom from eternal death apart from Him, for He has the keys to eternal life. Jesus is, indeed, the Father of Eternity.

Dr. Raymond Moody is a colleague and friend of Dr. Elizabeth Kubler-Ross, who channels a spirit guide. Shortly after she wrote the book *Death and Dying*, Dr. Moody also wrote a book, entitled *Life After Life*. In this book he speaks of near-death experiences and contacts with beings of light. There are numerous stories in his book about people who were greatly encouraged by these beings of light because they gave a certain spiritual enlightenment about what happens after death. Nothing is definitive in these stories, and there is no instruction on what comes after the light encounter. It's all very nebulous; and yet people are encouraged because somehow they feel that the after-death experience will be positive.

Now consider the comparison with Jesus. He is our enlightenment because His experience with death was complete, and His victory over death was thorough. He did not have a "near-death" experience and then come back to talk about ethereal beings of light. Jesus actually rose from the dead and returned to enlighten us concerning death and life after life. The so-called beings of light that Dr. Moody talks about pale into insignificance when compared to the glorious light of Christ. In the words of Jesus, "I am the way, and the truth, and the life; no one comes to the Father, but through Me" (John 14:6). Jesus alone is *Avi Ad*—Father of Eternity.

Whatever enlightenment the New Age spirit guides are promising is a deception that leads to greater darkness. They say that you can find the answers by looking within yourself. Now that is certainly misdirection because that's where the problems are, not the answers. Spirit guides do not know the way, they do not speak the truth, and they are not the dispensers of eternal life. The answers to life are not within us, and they are not in spirit guides—they are in Jesus Christ who is the Father of Eternity.

He is our entrance into eternity, and we can enter by no other way.

2. Jesus Christ Is Our Enjoyment of Eternity
When you think of holidays, what are your most pleasant memories? Apart from the exciting experiences, the food, and the

fun, most people would probably say that their most memorable times involved being with loved ones. Family and friends are really what make life enjoyable. The old adage explains it well— it doesn't matter where you go, and it doesn't matter what you do; what matters is who you're with.

The Bible tells us that this is what heaven will be like. Oh, there will be beautiful things to see and wonderful things to do, but the most incredible thing of all will be the absolute joy of who we're with. For many, the pleasure of once again being with loved ones who have departed prior to them will be an enjoyable part of the heavenly experience. But by far the most spectacular aspect of eternal life with God will be the sheer joy of living in the presence of Christ.

The disciples of Jesus were anxious about the future and emotionally distraught over the news that Jesus was going away. In His effort to comfort them, Jesus made them a promise:

> Let not your heart be troubled; you believe in God, believe also in Me. In my Father's house are many dwelling places; if it were not so, I would have told you; for I go to prepare a place for you. And if I go and prepare a place for you, I will come again, and receive you to Myself; that where I am, there you may be also.
>
> —JOHN 14:1-3

Jesus is highlighting the fact that He will be there with us in heaven. Just as the highlight of a holiday season is to be with family and friends, so our deepest sense of joy in the future life will be the pleasure of being with Christ. Jesus will be our chief enjoyment of eternity. We will forever look to Him as a child looks to his father.

Alfred Martin, in his commentary, speaking about the Father of Eternity, says this means "the One who nourishes and protects His own forever."[9] Matthew Henry writes of this name by saying, "His fatherly care of his people and tenderness towards them are everlasting."[10] David Garland adds this thought: He "will do for His own for an eternity what an earthly father would do for his children as long as he lived."[11]

What a glorious hope we have in Jesus Christ, our Father of Eternity! It is only through Him that we enter into eternal fellowship with God. But He is also the Person who will make our experience of eternity such a joy. We will not be abandoned to a meaningless existence, wandering forever alone. Oh, no! In contrast, we will spend it with Him as we enjoy the attention of His fatherly care. For He is our Father of Eternity.

WHAT DOES ALL OF THIS MEAN TO ME?

Isaiah has painted a descriptive picture for us of a very special Person whom the New Testament identifies as Jesus Christ. Here we have considered that His name is not only Wonderful Counselor and Mighty God, but also Father of Eternity. You may not have thought of Jesus in a fatherly role, but perhaps you are now encouraged to know that this is exactly who He is. He loves you as a father loves his child, and He cares for you in the same way a father cares for His children. He will guide you through the labyrinth of life into the safe harbor of eternity as you entrust your life to Him. And best of all, you will have the privilege of enjoying His wonderful, loving presence forever! All of this is wrapped up in the fact that He is your Father of Eternity.

As you reflect on these thoughts, let the Spirit of God encourage your heart with all that Christ is for you. Do you know Him as your personal Savior? If so, then He is your Father of Eternity. Are you aware that He wants to use your life as a channel of His grace to others? Now, that's something to get excited about! Have you looked to Him for guidance as you make the decisions of life and as you plan for your future? Unlike other spirit guides, He will lead into that which is true and right. And above all, rejoice in the fact that He has opened the door of eternity for you through His death on the cross for your sins and through His resurrection from the dead—because He is Father of Eternity.

WHEN THE WORLD WILL BE AT REST

An Introduction to the Czar of Peace

"... Prince of Peace."
ISAIAH 9:6

There is nothing in our world as elusive as peace. More than anything else, it seems, peace is at the top of everyone's list of concerns—personal peace, national peace, and global peace. Yet the world continues to be plagued with conflict and anxiety. Spin the globe, stop it at random with your finger, and most likely you will be pointing at a hot spot of tension and/or war. From Northern Ireland to the Balkans, from the Middle East and Iraq to the Korean peninsula, there is flagrant animosity and hostile intent. What is it about our world that makes peace so hard to attain? Everybody wants it, we get excited about the slightest possibility of finding it, and people march on the capitals of the world to demand it. Yet achieving peace is as frustrating as chasing shadows and grabbing sunbeams.

One of the foremost agendas of the New World Order and

the New Age Movement has been the pursuit of peace. Dave Hunt, who wrote the book *Global Peace and the Rise of Antichrist*, makes this observation: "Ecology and peace are the two great concerns that are sparking the new unity of all religions. Nothing else matters. Doctrinal beliefs are irrelevant. . . . It is astonishing not only what ungodly but what bizarre 'spirituality' the world is willing to embrace in its search for peace and ecological salvation."[1]

This is also true of the postmodern culture in general. The idea seems to be that if we can neutralize the tension inherent in conflicting ideas, then we can achieve ultimate peace. So everything is personalized and relativized. There is no such thing as *the* truth—only your truth and my truth. *Tolerance* is the byword of our culture, and no one can be critical of anyone else. In the process, it appears that we are being reduced as a society to politically correct morons. No one needs to think anymore— there's no reason to think. We are simply encouraged to experience our diverse world like enjoying the various flavors of ice cream at Baskin Robbins.

Yet it continues to be a mess out there. Look around—it's a dog-eat-dog world, isn't it? Everyone is out to get theirs, right? And they'll get yours too, if they can get away with it. The world is festering with conflict. Everywhere we look, it's person against person, nation against nation, culture against culture, ethnic group against ethnic group. The only way to ensure peace, it seems, is to have bigger weapons, better armies and navies, more nuclear weapons, and better defense systems. Face it—there is no peace on earth, only the temporary control of continual aggression.

So what's the answer? Well, one starlit night while shepherds were watching their flocks in the fields of Bethlehem, an angel from heaven unveiled the solution for peace in the world.

According to the ancient historian Dr. Luke, this is what the angel said:

> *Fear not: for, behold, I bring you good tidings of great joy, which shall be to all people. For unto you is born this day in the city of David a Saviour, which is Christ the Lord. And this shall be a sign unto you; Ye shall find the babe wrapped in swaddling clothes, lying in a manger. And suddenly there was with the angel a multitude of the heavenly host praising God, and saying, Glory to God in the highest, and on earth peace, good will toward men.*
>
> —LUKE 2:10-14, KJV

In this record of the angelic message to the shepherds, Dr. Luke linked the birth of the Child in swaddling clothes with the fulfillment of peace on earth. In a similar vein, the prophet Isaiah associated the virgin-born Child with a government of universal peace in the world. Let's review the verses again:

> *6 For a child will be born to us, a son will be given to us; and the government will rest on His shoulders; and His name will be called Wonderful Counselor, Mighty God, Eternal Father, Prince of Peace. 7 There will be no end to the increase of His government or of peace, on the throne of David and over his kingdom, to establish it and to uphold it with justice and righteousness from then on and forevermore. The zeal of the LORD of hosts will accomplish this.*
>
> —ISAIAH 9:6-7

We have been looking at the various aspects of the name that the Child will be called. Here we have come to the last couplet— "Prince of Peace." This does not just involve what this Person will do—bring peace to the earth. We will focus on *who He is* that makes possible what He will do.

As with the other three couplet designations, this name is also two words in the original Hebrew text, corresponding to the two English words. In the Hebrew we find the words, *Sar Shalom*—*Sar* ("Prince") and *Shalom* ("Peace"). He is *Sar Shalom*, Prince of Peace. These two words convey the entire hope of the world. So let's look at each word, as we have done with the previous compound names.

SAR — "PRINCE": PEACE IS FOUND IN THE PERSON OF GOD

Isaiah confronts us with a revolutionary thought concerning the source of peace. He assures us that peace is not merely a concept—it is a Person. It is to be found in a unique Prince, who is the Son of God.

The Hebrew word *sar* is a word that means "master, head, or chief," as well as "commander, ruler, leader, or noble." It is certainly well translated here by the word "Prince." Actually it is the Semitic equivalent of the word "czar," an ancient Russian ruler. The first word of this couplet, therefore, focuses our attention on a regal person—one with the power and authority to do something with regard to the cause of peace in the world.

As Messiah, the Prince Is God Incarnate

Who is this person, this Czar of Peace? In Isaiah's teaching, the Prince is none other than the long-awaited Messiah who is God in human flesh. You see, Isaiah has been building his case. Do you remember back in chapter 7 and verse 14 (we've looked at it often in this series of studies), where it says that the Lord will give a sign—a virgin will conceive and bear a Son, and they'll call His name Immanuel? Well, then you probably also remember that Immanuel means "God with us"—*Immanu* (with us) and *El*, the shortened form of *Elohim* (the God who created the universe). "With us . . . God," or "God with us," is what it means. Isaiah specifically points out that the virgin-born Child will be God Incarnate, or God in human flesh.

Then when Isaiah comes to chapter 9, verse 6, he adds the thought that the Child's name will be "Mighty God" (*El Gibbor*). Again, the Child is said to be *El*, the great God of Creation. So the Prince of Peace is really Mighty God; He is Immanuel—God with us.

Isaiah is saying that peace is not a charismatic plan crafted by clever politicians. Peace is not the collective will of a conglomerate of nations ruling the world from the East River in New York City. Peace is not the warm feelings of love generated by flower children sitting in a patch of daisies on a hillside. Peace is not the emergence of an Aquarian Age in the aligning of planets and stars. Peace is a Person! Peace is a glorious, majestic, all-wise, all-powerful Person who is Immanuel, the Creator of the universe. As the angel said to the shepherds long ago, if there is to be "peace, good will toward men" on earth, there must first be "glory to God in the highest."

In the pursuit of peace, our secular, humanistic society makes two fundamental mistakes. First, it denies the existence of a personal, infinite God; and second, it exalts the creature over the Creator.

1. They Deny the Existence of a Personal, Infinite God

If there is no God and there is no involvement of God in the affairs of men, then there is very little hope of lasting peace on earth. Man has had millennia of opportunity to prove himself as a peacemaker, and history proves that he has been a perennial failure. There has been temporary peace but only for short periods of time; it has never lasted. When there is no God to produce what man has never been able to accomplish, then the world is without a Helper. The world is simply drifting toward cosmic chaos, breakdown, and destruction. It is an exercise in futility. There can be momentary respite, but there can never be ultimate peace.

2. THEY EXALT THE CREATURE OVER THE CREATOR

A second mistake made by secular humanists is to assume that man is his own god. Some religious perspectives believe that men and women are evolving into gods, but the secular mind-set is simply that man is capable of determining his own destiny. Through advanced technology and creative thinking, it is believed, man will solve his own problems and find lasting peace.

Well, on the surface that sounds well and good, but there is something curiously irrational about it all. All history argues against the idea that mankind is getting better and is evolving into some kind of a super-species. There is as much inhumanity against humanity today as there has ever been, and advanced technology has simply given us more sophisticated ways of killing ourselves. Are we so foolish to think that sinful, self-centered, greedy, power-hungry men will bring peace to the earth? The solution of these men will be as corrupt as every other solution that has ever been offered to our planet. It is wishful thinking at best.

So why is there tension, anxiety, and a lack of peace in the world today? Well, the Bible explains it in a very straightforward way. It is because people have decided to ignore God and to cast off the moral restraints of His Law. It's as simple as that. Let's take a moment to go back to Psalm 2, which we considered earlier, and see exactly how God addresses this issue.

PSALM 2: WHY THERE IS NO PEACE IN THE WORLD

Psalm 2 begins with the word "why." That is *the* question everyone seems to be asking. "Why are the nations in an uproar, and the peoples devising a vain thing?" (v. 1). In other words, why is there international conflict and individual confusion? The nations are stirred up and restless, like a boiling pot of churning water. On an individual level, people are empty and frustrated to the point that they are questioning the very rationale of life. The psalmist sees that there is no peace in the world, and he asks the obvious question, "Why?"

The answer quickly flows from his pen. "The kings of the earth take their stand," he says, "and the rulers take counsel together against the LORD and against His Anointed: 'Let us tear their fetters apart, and cast away their cords from us!'" (vv. 2-3). In other words, the governmental leaders and policy-makers of our society have decided that they do not want to be accountable to God, and their counsel is to get rid of Him and His "Anointed" (this is the Hebrew word *masiah*, Messiah). They are determined to throw off the boundaries and restraints of divine law so that they are free to do whatever they like. These greedy, power-hungry officials want to be their own gods so they can determine their own selfish destinies, as well as the destinies of the people they lead. In turn, the people become frustrated with the injustice and unrighteousness of their environments. It is all a mad cycle of depravity. And this, according to God's Word, is the explanation for the lack of peace in our world. As the kids say, "Duh!" What did you expect when you thumb your nose at God? This isn't rocket science—it's just plain common sense.

Now you need to understand that God's purpose is not thwarted when puny men shake their fists toward heaven. Psalm 2 goes on to describe God's reaction to this human mutiny: "He who sits in the heavens laughs, the Lord scoffs at them. Then He will speak to them in His anger and terrify them in His fury: 'But as for Me, I have installed My King upon Zion, My holy mountain'" (vv. 4-6). God is merely biding His time, waiting for the appropriate moment to announce that enough is enough. At that time He will put an end to all rebellion and enthrone His King, the Anointed Messiah, upon the earth. This One is the virgin-born Child of Isaiah's prophecy who will have the government upon His shoulder. Then, and only then, will there be peace on earth.

So the next time you are tempted to ask, "Why is the world in such a mess?" think of this Psalm and reflect on its simple but profound answer. Man does not have the solution to the lack of peace in the world; on the contrary, he is the reason there is no peace in the world. That's the way it has always been, and that's the way it will always be until Messiah returns. It is the height of naiveté to think that things could be otherwise. You see, only God can bring peace to the individual heart and to the nations of the world. The Prince of Isaiah's prophecy is the Anointed Messiah, and as the Messiah, He is God. That is why His name will be called Prince of Peace.

As Creator, the Prince Has All Authority

When the Prince of Peace rules on the earth and the government is upon His shoulder, there will be an unprecedented time of peace pervading the world. Isaiah puts it this way, "There will be no end to the increase of *His* government or of peace" (Isa. 9:7). Think of it—"no end to . . . peace." The idea here is that His government will encompass the world, and peace will follow wherever He rules. His government will be known not only for its justice and righteousness, but also for its all-inclusive peace. There will be *individual peace*, and there will be *global peace* because of the presence of the Prince of Peace.

So, how will Christ accomplish this? Well, for any common man this would be an impossible task to be sure, but the Czar of Peace is not a common man. He is the unique Son of God. His name is *El Gibbor* (Mighty God), and He is *Immanuel* (God with us). *El*, you remember, is *Elohim*; and *Elohim* is the Creator of the universe ("In the beginning God [*Elohim*] created the heavens and the earth" (Gen. 1:1). As Creator, therefore, He has the infinite ability and supreme authority to accomplish whatever He designs to do. As Isaiah put it, "The zeal of the LORD of hosts will accomplish this" (9:7).

The Kingdom Age will be a new creation. This is actually what Christ produces now in the life of every believer: "Therefore if any man is in Christ, *he is* a new creature; the old things passed away; behold new things have come" (2 Cor. 5:17). The individual confusion spoken of in Psalm 2 is replaced by a supernatural peace in the lives of those who trust Him (Phil. 4:6-7). It is nothing short of amazing to observe how He can transform a person's life! And that is exactly what the Bible says He will do with the natural world as well. Peter was excited when he wrote, "But according to His promise we are looking for new heavens and a new earth, in which righteousness dwells" (2 Pet. 3:13). This is the real hope of the world. It is the promise of a Kingdom Age on the earth.

Elohim has the ability to re-create and regenerate everything that He touches because He is the Creator. He can just speak the word and it happens (Ps. 33:9). What a glorious thing! You see, He has all authority to do that. So creating a kingdom of universal peace is no problem for Him.

Now in both cases, whether it's personal or global, it is the Person of Jesus Christ who accomplishes the peace. He's the One who makes the new creature, and He's the One who makes the new creation. Everything He does is characterized by peace because He is the Prince of Peace. The apostle Paul put it this way: "For He Himself is our peace" (Eph. 2:14).

There is another aspect to this, however. Whenever anyone engages in a project of renovation and renewal, there is always the challenge of effectively removing the old worn-out parts. A few years ago my wife and I bought an older house that was a "fixer-upper." One of the projects was to remove the worn-out flooring in order to re-carpet the house. The old carpet was really bad—soiled and stained from years of use. But in several rooms there was the added problem of animal odor. Two cats and a dog had staked out a corner of each room as their personal latrine. It was awful. The carpet and pad were putrid, but the problem didn't stop there. The animal urine had soaked into the concrete sub-floor so that the room continued to smell even with the carpet removed. So I spent hours with a two-pound sledge hammer and a concrete chisel removing the upper layers of concrete. Then I had to patch and resurface the sub-floor before we could lay the new flooring. The biggest part of the project, by far, was getting rid of the bad stuff before installing that which was new and better.

Now the Bible teaches that this is a major concern in the matters of personal and global renewal as well. Peace is elusive because of all the bad stuff that exists to disrupt it. But the Prince of Peace not only has the authority and power to create a new heart and a new world, He also has the authority to put away all evil. Control and authority over evil have always been the key to creating peace.

In the days of ancient Rome, the Empire was known for its *Pax Romana*, the peace of Rome. During this era there was a general peace in the Roman Empire, and individuals could traverse the Mediterranean world in relative safety. It was one of the better times of history in the ancient world, but the *Pax Romana* was secured and maintained by the point of the spear and the edge of the sword. Moreover, the Caesars ruled with totalitarian oppression. Rome's corrupt and often brutal control was the price of peace.

It is no different today, although the names have changed. America is a peaceful nation, and we are struggling to ensure peace in the world. But control and authority are the issues of the day. For the first time in our nation's history, we have a Cabinet-level Department of Homeland Security. Controlling evil and thwarting aggression are priority concerns for both our law enforcement personnel at home and our military abroad. We're working hard at peace, but controlling evil has continued to be an enormous task.

So again we ask the same question: What is the ultimate answer for peace in the world? And again the answer is the same—it is the authority of God imposed on the earth. Appealing to Psalm 2 once more, we read of the authority of the Messiah, the Anointed One, to put down all evil as He comes to establish the Kingdom Age. Jehovah God says, "Ask of Me, and I will surely give the nations as Thine inheritance, and the *very* ends of the earth as Thy possession. Thou shalt break them with a rod of iron, Thou shalt shatter them like earthenware" (vv. 8-9). Notice the authority and power. Notice the control. It is God's control over the earth—and that's why there will be peace, as evil is put away and as righteousness reigns. That is how peace will become pervasive in the earth.

You see, the more we study Scripture, the more we realize that peace is a Person who has all of the inherent authority of the Creator-God. Just before Jesus ascended into heaven after His resurrection from the dead, He said to His disciples, "All authority has been given to Me in heaven and on earth" (Matt. 28:18). Jesus has all authority, and that's why He is the author of personal and global peace. He is *Sar Shalom*—the Prince of Peace. All who acknowledge Him as their Savior from sin and evil, all who pledge their allegiance to Him as their Lord, will know this peace. We can know the peace of salvation now as He makes us a new creation; and we can have the sure hope of peace in the Kingdom Age in keeping with His promise of a new heavens and a new earth (Isa. 65:17). He is the Czar of Peace.

SHALOM—"PEACE": PEACE IS OBTAINED AS A PROVISION FROM GOD

As we turn our focus from the word "Prince" to the word "Peace," we need to understand that peace is a provision obtained from God. The word translated "Peace" in the name Prince of Peace is the Hebrew word *shalom*. This is a beautiful word in the Hebrew language with a variety of meanings. If you go to Israel and listen to Jewish people talk, you will hear them saying "*shalom*" on many occasions. For instance, when people greet one another they will say, "*Shalom*." Then when they leave, they will also say, "*Shalom*." It is both "hello" and "good-bye" and carries with it the idea of "best wishes." In fact, the overall concept seems to be, "May you have good health and be prosperous in life." In all of the various meanings the root idea is one of peace and prosperity.

The principal city of Israel is Jerusalem. If it weren't for tension with the Arabs, Jerusalem would be the capital of the Israeli nation. But for now at least Tel Aviv is where the other nations of the world do business with Israel. Nevertheless, even though there is very little peace in Jerusalem, that is what "Jerusalem" means. The name Jerusalem is formed by combining *Jeru* (*yeru*—"city") and *salem* (*shalom*—"peace"). Jerusalem is the City of Peace, but over the years it has known anything but peace.

A few years ago there was a biased bit of humor that circulated with regard to Israel. The thought was that Israel really *is* interested in peace—they want a piece of Jordan, they want a piece of Syria, and they want a piece of Egypt. Well, that's not the way it really is because in recent years Israel has been willing to give away land for peace. They are desperate for peace, and yet Jerusalem is not *Yeru-shalom*. It's not a city of peace, and hasn't been for years.

Now the reason for this lack of peace according to Isaiah is that Israel has not turned its national heart toward the Prince of Peace. The angelic message to the shepherds in Bethlehem was, " . . . and on earth peace, good will toward men" (Luke 2:14, KJV), but that was because the Prince of Peace had been born and was right then cradled in a manger. The more literal reading of the angel's message is captured by the New American Standard Bible, which says, ". . . and on earth peace among men with whom He is pleased." Or consider the New International Version: " . . . and on earth peace to men on whom his favor rests." You see, it is not just a blanket of peace hovering over the earth, but peace to those whose response to the Prince of Peace is well-pleasing to God. This is obviously true in the realm of personal peace as well. We have to respond to Christ and trust Him before He will give us His peace. He doesn't just automatically dispense peace irrespective of our willingness to trust Him. So there is good reason why there is no peace in Jerusalem and a serious void of peace in the world. There has been a general rejection of Jesus Christ as Savior and Lord by both the Jews and the world; and where the Prince of Peace is rejected, there is no peace.

1. It Is Frustrating to Pursue Peace Without Christ

Pursuing peace apart from Christ is frustrating and futile. This is reflected in the history of Israel leading up to the context of Isaiah 9. In the early days of the monarchy, when Saul was Israel's first king, there was constant war with the Philistines, who were the original Palestinians (*Palestine* comes from the word *Philistine*). Then King David came along and defeated all of the enemies who surrounded the nation, making it possible for Solomon to reign with a relative degree of peace. The Hebrew spelling of Solomon is *Shlomo*, which comes from the word *shalom*. Solomon's name means "peaceful one," and it was under Solomon that Israel enjoyed a significant period of peace.

But here is where the story turns bad again. Solomon neglected the Lord and allowed his many wives to turn him away from the worship of Jehovah God. The nation of Israel gradually became more and more corrupt, so that after his death there was civil war in the land. Solomon's son Rehoboam ended up with a small piece of the nation in the south; and Jeroboam, a man Solomon had once trusted, took the lion's share of ten tribes and split off to form the northern kingdom. From that time on, there was major unrest between the two factions and increased harassment from their enemies. It had become a royal mess in Israel.

We then come to the time of Isaiah—a prophet to the southern kingdom who wrote of the deplorable conditions in Israel. The first verses of chapter 9 say that the nation was a dark place filled with gloom and despair. The people had turned their backs on God, and there was no peace in the land. You can put it down as one of the unalterable laws of spirituality that if there is no peace *with* God, then there is no peace *of* God. Isaiah says an interesting thing in this regard later in his book:

"Peace, peace to him who is far and to him who is near,"
Says the LORD, "and I will heal him."
But the wicked are like the tossing sea,
For it cannot be quiet,
And its waters toss up refuse and mud.
"There is no peace," says my God, "for the wicked."

ISAIAH 57:19-21

You see, as Isaiah wrote, Israel was without peace and in imminent danger of invasion from Assyria because the Jews were wicked in the eyes of God. Jeremiah would later record the destruction of Jerusalem and the Temple by Babylon and the deportation of thousands of people to the land of Mesopotamia (modern-day Iraq). Peace had turned away from them because they had turned away from God.

Jumping ahead to the world's future, the Bible teaches that the same scenario will transpire in "the last days." The Antichrist will offer the world a contrived peace based upon false worship and a rejection of Christ. The apostle Paul wrote of this, saying,

> *Now as to the times and the epochs, brethren, you have no need of anything to be written to you. For you yourselves know full well that the day of the Lord will come just like a thief in the night. While they are saying, "Peace and safety!" then destruction will come upon them suddenly like birth pangs upon a woman with child; and they shall not escape.*
>
> —1 THESS. 5:1-3

People in that day will think they have peace, but it will be an elusive peace. They will think they are safe, but it will be harm in the guise of safety. What an awful thing that will be! Having rejected Christ, they will have forfeited their opportunity to have lasting peace. Perhaps you have seen the bumper sticker, "No Christ, no Peace—know Christ, know peace." That pretty much sums it up.

You see, people are looking for peace in all the wrong places. The angelic announcement in Bethlehem of "peace on earth" has not yet been fulfilled because the world has rejected the Son of God who is the Prince of Peace. Instead they beat Him, spat in His face, and drove nails into His hands and feet. They put a crown of thorns on His head and mocked the Czar of Peace. No wonder peace is so elusive. People are looking everywhere but to Christ. And they are discovering that it is frustrating to pursue peace *without* Christ.

So let me ask you a personal question. Has peace been elusive for you? Are you anxious and troubled? Are you fighting life and defending your turf? Are you angry and bitter, striking out at those who have hurt you? Then you have not come to Christ and opened your heart to the Prince of Peace or you are not walking with Him. You may praise Him with your lips on Sunday, but you have locked Him out of your heart in life. Listen, wherever He is, there *will* be peace. Commit your life to Him, and let Him rule in your heart. Remember, it is frustrating to pursue peace without Christ!

2. It Is Fulfilling to Experience Peace with Christ

If it is frustrating to pursue peace without Christ, it is also fulfilling to experience peace with Christ. Isaiah is helping us understand that ultimate peace is associated with a Person, the Prince of Peace, and experiencing that peace is directly related to whether or not we have a personal relationship with that Person. Furthermore, the government of the Kingdom Age will be a government of peace because the government will rest upon

His shoulder. Whether it is global peace or personal peace, it is all associated with who He is.

So then, what kind of peace are we talking about? Isaiah gives us the answer later in his book, where he reveals that it is perfect peace: "Thou wilt keep *him* in perfect peace, *whose* mind *is* stayed *on thee*: because he trusteth in thee" (26:3, KJV). Wow! What a great promise! Perfect peace—there's nothing shabby about that! Actually, the Hebrew phrase here is exceedingly strong. The word for peace (*shalom*) is simply repeated, so that the phrase is "*shalom shalom*," or "the peace of peace." Jesus is called "the King of kings, and the Lord of lords" (1 Tim. 6:15), and the peace He gives according to Isaiah is the peace of peace. Whenever there is a reduplication of words in Hebrew, an emphasis is put on the ultimate nature of the word. As Jesus is the King of all kings, so the peace He gives is the peace of all peace. It is indeed *perfect* peace.

This is the very peace Paul was referring to in Philippians 4:6-7: "Be anxious for nothing, but in everything by prayer and supplication, with thanksgiving, let your requests be made known to God; and the *peace of God, which surpasses all understanding*, will guard your hearts and minds through Christ Jesus" (NKJV, emphasis mine). Now, isn't that amazing? The peace that Jesus Christ gives is so phenomenal that you won't be able to explain it. And it is so powerful that it will totally soothe your mind and comfort your heart. There is complete relief in the peace of Christ because it is a pervasive peace. That is why He is called the Prince of Peace—because in Him there is perfect peace, the kind that surpasses your ability to comprehend.

Without question, this is the very peace H. G. Spafford discovered when facing a series of horrific events. His story is well-known and has been repeated often, but perhaps it bears repeating again. Horatio Gates Spafford lost everything he owned in the great Chicago fire of 1871. Standing in the ashes of his possessions, he decided to send his wife and four daughters on a ship to England while he remained behind on urgent business in Chicago. Feeling relieved that they were removed from the devastation, he plunged into the task of recovery. Little did he know that a tragic ship accident in the North Atlantic would deprive him still further of his beloved daughters. Shortly afterward, he received a telegram from his wife in England with two difficult words, "saved alone."

Immediately, H. G. Spafford booked passage on another boat to join his grieving wife in Wales. As the ship skimmed through the ocean waters, Spafford asked the captain to wake him when they passed over the very spot where his daughters Tanetta, Maggie, Annie, and Bessie (along with 222 others) had gone down. Late one night there was a knock on his cabin door to inform him of the approaching spot. He made his way to the deck, and peering down into the dark waters, he wrote the immortal words of our beloved hymn: "When peace, like a river, attendeth my way, when sorrows like sea billows roll; whatever my lot, thou hast taught me to say, 'It is well, it is well with my soul.'"[2] Horatio Gates Spafford knew something of the perfect peace that passes understanding, which only Jesus can bestow.

There are many illustrations of people who have experienced this wonderful peace that I could share. For instance, I think of a dear lady whom my wife and I knew earlier in our ministry and continue to admire. She had a wayward son who was profligate and irresponsible, even though he was married. He was totally insensitive to his family and eventually divorced his wife while continuing to live his selfish lifestyle. This lady (his mother) carried a heavy burden in her heart not only for her son, but also for her daughter-in-law.

During the time she was going through all of this, I received a call one afternoon. With an almost apologetic tone in her voice for disturbing me, she related through deep feelings of emotion that the state police had just informed her that her husband had been killed in an accident while driving his truck in foggy conditions. As her pastor, I ministered to her as best I could; but somehow her strength in the Lord seemed to make all my words of comfort unnecessary.

A few years later one of her daughters married a Christian young man, and there was an experience of joy for this godly woman. My wife and I were so happy for her as she later delighted in the birth of several grandchildren. But then disappointment reared its ugly head again as this son-in-law admitted unfaithfulness to his wife. Heavy pornography had led to illicit sexual encounters with prostitutes, and when his sinful behavior was discovered, he remained unrepentant. He proceeded to choose his wicked lifestyle over their marriage, and he walked away from his wife and children. It was a devastating situation for this woman who had already experienced so much pain; and for her heartbroken daughter, it felt worse than death. To this day, this man continues to take pleasure in his sin.

What is truly inspiring in the midst of all of this is how this lady and her defrauded daughter found a healing peace in Christ. They turned *to* the Lord instead of *away* from Him and discovered in a tangible way that He is truly the Prince of Peace. This woman and her daughter have gone through unbelievable trouble and heartache—sorrows like rolling sea billows. Yet they have remained loving and gentle as servants of Christ. Even now as I think of these women, I thank the Lord that here are living examples that Christ is true to His Word—He is the great peace-giver.

So, do you get it? The good news is that peace is available, but you must look for it in the right place. You won't find it in your circumstances, and you won't find it in the empty promises of well-meaning people. You will only find lasting and genuine peace when you accept Jesus as your Savior and when you walk with Him as your Lord. He is *Sar Shalom*. He is the Prince of Peace.

NAME ABOVE ALL NAMES

Isaiah's words are a prophecy. He entices us with things yet to come. "For a child will be born to us, a son will be given to us" (9:6). Our interest peaks as we contemplate the incredible impact of this sensational Person upon the world. The fact that His name will be called Wonderful Counselor, Mighty God, Eternal Father, and Prince of Peace only heightens our expectation to exalted levels of impatience. "When?" we cry. "When will He come?"

We finger our way forward in the Word of God, past the great prophets of the Captivity and Restoration, until we break the cover of the New Covenant. Matthew is the bridge from the Old to the New, and there we read in his opening chapter that the promised Child has been born. It is the very Child of Isaiah's prophecy, we are told, and His name is Jesus (Matt. 1:20-23).

What a life Jesus lived—truly amazing in every respect. Over and over in His interactions with people we see Him as the *Wonderful Counselor*. And the miracles! My, what miracles; they leave you breathless with wonder. Truly here is *Mighty God*! He promised eternal life to all who would believe in Him. Can anyone seriously question that He is the Father of Eternity, the *Eternal Father*? As we read on, our hearts beat faster as we see Him arrested, tried, and crucified. Yet there is a special tranquillity about His life in the midst of it all that assures us that He is the *Prince of Peace*. Never has any man died with greater dignity and a more impressive repose. In the end we stand and applaud as He rises from the dead, proving that He is an effective Savior and worthy dispenser of eternal life.

But that is not the end! It is only the beginning of the end. For as this unique Person of heavenly origin ascends back into heaven, He promises to return again to Planet Earth as the King of kings (Acts 1:9-11). It is here that we understand that Isaiah's prophecy has only been partially fulfilled. There is more. The government part is yet to come—when "the government will rest on His shoulders" and when "there will be no end to the increase of *His* government or of peace" (Isa. 9:6-7). We rush on to the end of the book, and suddenly we are aghast. With John we fall on our faces with awe and quiver at the touch of Jesus' almighty hand (Rev. 1:17).

The brilliance of His white robe reflecting the sheer glory of His magnificent presence is stunning, and we are overwhelmed with trembling joy. A golden breastplate wraps itself around His powerful chest in a show of regal splendor, and His feet glow with the fiery intensity of metal in a blast furnace. It is then that our attention is drawn upward to His face, where we are mesmerized with breathtaking wonder. His head and His hair are white like wool, like newly fallen snow before it is soiled. And His eyes—who can look at His eyes?—for they are penetrating lasers piercing the inner soul and laying bare the very thoughts and intentions of the heart. A blinding aura radiates from His visage, and we are sure that we are gazing into the strength of the noonday sun. He speaks, and the thunder of His voice causes tremors that vibrate like the quaking of the earth beneath our feet. It is then that we see the sword—a sharp two-edged sword— proceeding out of His mouth. Lightning that accompanies the thunder of His voice will surgically decimate His foes. He is awesome—incredibly awesome! As the warrior of the Godhead, He is postured to descend upon the earth (Rev. 1:12-18).

As we flip the pages to the end, we fumble with inadequate words to describe the sheer magnificence of Christ's return to the earth. The authority of His voice, the strength of His presence, and the radiance of His glory are more than words will allow. Even the great white stallion upon which He sits is grander than any beast among men. Rider and war steed are as one as they descend through the clouds upon the mayhem of earth. The slaughter at Armageddon has already exceeded historic proportions; but now the kings of the East and the tyrant of Jerusalem controlled by the spirit of Antichrist turn their attention to the sky. A common enemy of their combined evil forces is hovering over their heads, and they realize in their hearts that the hunter has become the hunted. Their weapons are puny and insignificant against the spiritual forces of heaven; yet they persist in shouting blasphemies and raging threats. In a moment of time modern technology is relegated to obsolescence.

Then the Almighty Son of God opens His mouth, and a sharp two-edged sword pierces the atmosphere like a sizzling bolt of lightning surgically excising the cancerous evil from the earth. Judgment Day has come, and there is no hiding from His searching omniscience. The Child of Isaiah's prophecy has returned, and the government of Planet Earth is finally and forever on His shoulder (Rev. 19:11-21).

The process of renovation begins as the glorious Messiah reaches out with His creative hands to touch the scorched earth with His regenerative powers. New life buds forth from the ashes, and the desert begins to blossom like a rose. There's a new freshness in the air, and crystal-clear waters once again begin to flow in life-giving abundance. The curse has been lifted, and pollution is gone. Carnivorous animals have suddenly become herbivorous, and dangerous species are now benign. All of creation has awakened to a new day, and even the trees of the fields clap their hands. It's as God intended it to be when He first created the earth. The effects of sin are gone, and righteousness now prevails. Peace blankets the globe like oil upon troubled waters, and all instruments of war have been turned to productive use. The Prince of Peace has come, and the world is rejoicing (Isa. 11:6-9; 55:6-13; 65:17-25).

We hesitate to close the book, but reality presses upon us, and we realize that what shall be is not yet. Nevertheless, we are assured that Isaiah's words are true and sure. A glorious day is coming when the virgin-born Son who is our Savior will also reign on the earth as Lord of all. So we patiently wait and work for His Kingdom by introducing more people to His Gospel. And while we wait, we worship Him whose name is Wonderful Counselor, Mighty God, Eternal Father, Prince of Peace. His name is indeed *a name above all names*!

> *Therefore also God highly exalted Him, and bestowed on Him the name which is above every name, that at the name of Jesus every knee should bow, of those who are in heaven, and on earth, and under the earth, and that every tongue should confess that Jesus Christ is Lord, to the glory of God the Father.*
>
> —PHIL. 2:9-11

NOTES

CHAPTER ONE
NOT LIKE ANY OTHER

1. Bruce J. Nicholls, ed., *The Unique Christ in Our Pluralistic World* (Carlisle, UK and Grand Rapids, MI: Paternoster Press/Baker Book House, 1994), p. 7.
2. Thomas A. Harris, M.D., *I'm OK, You're OK* (New York: Avon Books, 1973).
3. Nicholls, *The Unique Christ in Our Pluralistic World*, p. 7.
4. Ibid., p. 14.
5. Ibid., p. 11.
6. Constance E. Cumbey, *The Hidden Dangers of the Rainbow* (Shreveport, LA: Huntington House, 1983), p. 13.
7. Texe Marrs, *Dark Secrets of the New Age* (Wheaton, IL: Crossway Books, 1987), p. 59.
8. Genesis 24:43; Exodus 2:8; Psalm 68:25; Proverbs 30:19; Song of Solomon 1:3; 6:8; Isaiah 7:14.

CHAPTER TWO
THE ULTIMATE RULER OF THE WORLD

1. John Steinbeck, in eds. Susan Shillinglaw and Jackson J. Benson, *America and Americans and Selected Nonfiction* (New York: Penguin Putnam, 2002), p. 403.

    Now we face the danger which in the past has been most destructive to the human: success—plenty, comfort, and ever-increasing leisure. No dynamic people has ever survived these dangers.

2. *The International Thesaurus of Quotations,* comp. Eugene Ehrlich and Marshall DeBruhl (New York: Harper Collins Publishers, 1996), p. 528.
3. George Orwell, *Animal Farm* (New York: Alfred A. Knopf, 1993).
4. Ibid., p. 16.
5. Ibid., p. 71.
6. Ibid., p. 44.
7. Ibid., p. 59.
8. Ibid., p. 88.

CHAPTER THREE
THAT'S AN UNUSUAL NAME

1. W. A. Criswell, *Isaiah—An Exposition* (Grand Rapids, MI: Zondervan Publishing House, 1977), p. 86.
2. Merrill F. Unger, *Unger's Commentary on the Old Testament, Volume II, Isaiah-Malachi* (Chicago: Moody Press, 1981), pp. 1167-1168.
3. H. E. Dana and Julius R. Mantey, *A Manual Grammar of the Greek New Testament* (New York: Macmillan, 1955), p. 149.
4. *Webster's New World Dictionary of the American Language,* Second College Edition (New York: Simon and Schuster, 1986).

CHAPTER FOUR
UNRAVELING THE MESS

1. W. E. Vine, *Isaiah—Prophecies, Promises, Warnings* (Grand Rapids, MI: Zondervan Publishing House, 1971), p. 43.
2. C. F. Keil and Franz Delitzsch, *Commentary on the Old Testament, Vol. VII—Isaiah* (Grand Rapids, MI: William B. Eerdmans, 1973), p. 251.
3. Ibid., p. 252.
4. Edward J. Young, *The Book of Isaiah, Volume I* (Grand Rapids, MI: William B. Eerdmans, 1965), p. 333.
5. Merrill F. Unger, *Unger's Commentary on the Old Testament, Vol. II—Isaiah-Malachi* (Chicago: Moody Press, 1981), p. 1168.
6. John Martin, "Isaiah," in eds. John F. Walvoord and Roy B. Zuck, *The Bible Knowledge Commentary, Volume I* (Wheaton, IL: Victor Books/Scripture Press, 1985), p. 1053.
7. D. David Garland, *Isaiah—A Study Guide Commentary* (Grand Rapids, MI: Zondervan Publishing House, 1968), p. 32.
8. Neil Postman, *Amusing Ourselves to Death* (New York: Penguin Books, 1986), p. 63.

CHAPTER FIVE
"YOU AIN'T SEEN NOTHIN' YET"

1. Vance Porter, *The Orlando Sentinel,* letter to the editor, January 31, 1991, p. A14.
2. John Martin, "Isaiah," in eds. John F. Walvoord and Roy B. Zuck, *The Bible Knowledge Commentary* (Wheaton, IL: Victor Books/Scripture Press, 1985), p. 1053.

3. F. C. Jennings, *Studies in Isaiah* (Neptune, NJ: Loizeaux Brothers, 1935), p. 117.
4. Horatius Bonar, *True Revivals and the Men God Uses* (London: Evangelical Press), p. 15.

CHAPTER SIX
THE MASTER OF THE KEYS

1. Tal Brooke, *When the World Will Be as One* (Eugene, OR: Harvest House, 1989), p. 22.
2. Ibid.
3. Ibid., p. 23.
4. Jon Klimo, *Channeling* (Berkeley, CA: North Atlantic Books, 1998), p. 1.
5. "Security," an old Swedish hymn.
6. "Channels Only," twentieth-century hymn, lyrics by Mary E. Maxwell, music by Ada Rose Gibbs.
7. J. Weingreen, *A Practical Grammar for Classical Hebrew*, 2nd ed. (Oxford: Oxford University Press, 1959), p. 44.
8. Merrill F. Unger, *Unger's Commentary on the Old Testament, Vol. II, Isaiah-Malachi* (Chicago: Moody Press, 1981), p. 1168.
9. Alfred Martin, *Isaiah—"The Salvation of Jehovah"* (Chicago: Moody Press, 1956), p. 42.
10. Matthew Henry, *Matthew Henry's Commentary on the Whole Bible, Vol. IV—Isaiah to Malachi* (Old Tappan, NJ: Fleming H. Revell), p. 60.
11. D. David Garland, *Isaiah—A Study Guide Commentary* (Grand Rapids, MI: Zondervan Publishing House, 1968), p. 32.

CHAPTER SEVEN
WHEN THE WORLD WILL BE AT REST

1. Dave Hunt, *Global Peace and the Rise of Antichrist* (Eugene, OR: Harvest House, 1990), p. 174.
2. Kenneth W. Osbeck, *Amazing Grace: 366 Inspiring Hymn Stories for Daily Devotions* (Grand Rapids, MI: Kregel Publications, 1990), p. 202.

Scripture Index

GENERAL INDEX